Dedicated to Tricia and the whole family.....

terry jones catching the moment

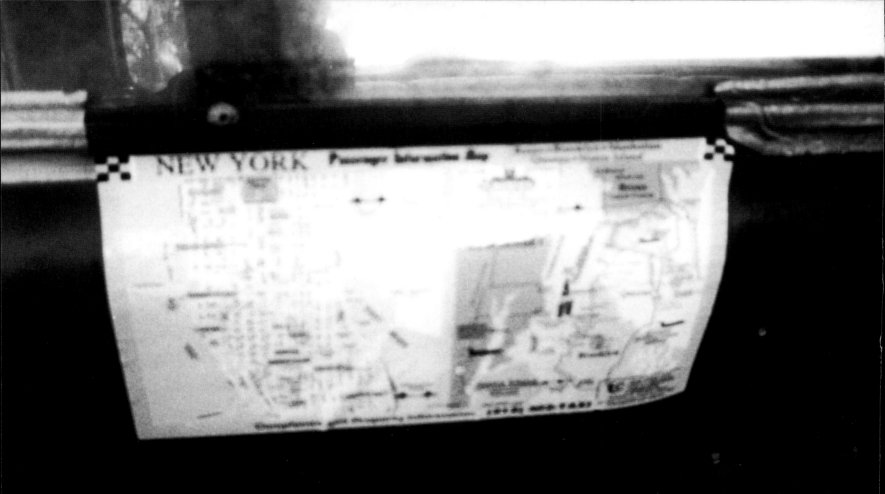

10 3 ! 96

" I'll take chances with covers. With chance there is always an element of risk.    My covers don't

ISBN 1 86154 010 8

Distributed world-wide and by direct mail through Internos Books 12 Percy Street, London W1P 9FB

Distribution in USA by Gingko Press Inc

Distribution in Japan by Tuttle Shokai Inc

Distribution in Singapore, Honk Kong, Thailand, Malaysia by Page One

neccessarily follow the commercial rules".

8

"I've taken chances with covers. With chance there is always an element of risk, so my covers don't follow the commercial rules."

Since Terry Jones first made an impact at "Vanity Fair" in the 1970, he has gone on to work for key European, American and Japanese publications and clients, mainly in the fashion industry. This book includes his choice of work from all of them: "Vogue" (UK), "Donna" (Italy), "Sportswear International" (Europe), Fiorucci (Italy), Esprit (USA), Fire and Ice (Germany) and "i-D" which he founded in 1980. Along the way Terry Jones has shown a rare ability to nurture new talent at the start of their careers. Amongst others, Oliviero Toscani, Nick Knight, Juergen Teller, Dylan Jones and Caryn Franklin. The impact of his work, which celebrates the energetic and the eccentric, has been unique, prompting not only key players in the creative industries but also his wider audience, the magazine-reading public, to explore new forms of self-expression. Wordsmith Perry Haines set the slogan style of the early issues, in his words: "Fashion is the way you walk, talk, dance and prance. It isn't what, but how you wear clothes that counts". Summer 1996 and I'm in Chicago, en route to the Canadian Rockies via Toronto, where I'll see my sister for two days before shooting another 'real life adventure' for Fire and Ice. Last night I had dinner with an old friend, Michael Conrad, the man who got me into advertising. I tried to

explain the idea behind this book, and what I told him may help you to navigate these pages.
"Catching the moment" was conceived after an editor from the publishing house which produced my design manual, "wink", came over to discuss a reprint. I explained that "wink" was intended as an instruction book of instant techniques and was already history, because instant is only relative to the moment in which it was done. Also it only showed one aspect of my role as an art director.
"Catching the moment" is intended to illustrate my aims as a director of communications. The job descriptions - art director, creative director, commercial artist, editor, publisher, dog handler, butcher, baker, shit maker, cheese shaker, whatever! - don't explain it. It's about working with other people - collaborators - to produce a result.
It's a year later and Terry's still defining "Catching the moment". While he's laying out the book he's making connections between words and images which he has created and helped to create. As the deadline looms, so much new stuff is happening...and he just can't stop the edit.
Things that made sense a year ago when the plan for the book was first discussed, seem less relevant now. I've recognised that the connections which produce "Catching the moment" are rarely historic. They're anecdotal and personal, sparked by memories or recollections. Or they're graphic concepts which link eras and reveal an evolution of ideas. Whether intentionally or not, the design of this book is not simply about projects I've been involved in but

has become a map of the way I work. This is probably in part because I have been living with it for so long; first as a concept, and then in the long process of production. I feel that it has absorbed a lot of the chaos and the structure of my working methods. There are always reasons behind choices, but sometimes, over time, those original lines of connection dissolve.

Today many art directors don't art direct they just get pictures in from a photographer and do layouts. That's why I want to publish a book about my approach to art direction and how it's evolved over the last twenty years. There was a period in the mid-70s at "Vogue" when I asked photographers to shoot on large format cameras, 5x4 and 10x8, and Bailey and Toscani were particularly creative at it. We messed around with all types of film and different cameras, and used heavy cut-out montage and joke backgrounds.

Oliviero Toscani, creative director, Benetton: "I first worked with Terry at 'Vanity Fair' and then he moved to 'Vogue' but he wasn't a 'Vogue' victim. He wanted to try new things, and at that time British 'Vogue' was different from the others, it had a different pace. We tried new girls, and we were the first to publish a Polaroid. He's a good salesman and could talk the editor round, so we got certain pictures through that weren't obviously 'Vogue'. Terry is of that breed of art directors that doesn't exist any more, the kind who leaves you alone in a white room with a fly and immediately you start to chase it. I like his way of destroying with graphics and I pushed him to put type on top of my pictures. Photographers are kind of blind people, they see in another way, and are blind in judging their pictures. He understood that and added the view."

One particular "Vogue" cover of Bianca Jagger, was never shot as a cover. Eric Bowman, who took the photograph, was an illustrator, but he had a good eye and was a social sort of person, in with the celebrities. I got him photographing and gave him a really good technical assistant. He did a shoot that was only meant to be a story inside, but I cropped the shit out of one of the photographs and put it on the cover. It was a 35mm transparency of Bianca photographed sitting in the top balcony at the opera. I just liked the idea of the sparkle in her eye. That wasn't the normal sort of thing you did for a "Vogue" cover.

The final straw at "Vogue", when I actually decided to leave, was over the cover of the Diamond Jubilee issue. I wanted to turn the cover into a window, so I asked for an engraving of the word VOGUE to be made in glass, and had it photographed. It took two weeks for a specialist crystal glass cutter in Ireland to engrave the letters into 8mm-thick plate glass. It took another week for "Vogue" photographer James Mortimer to get the right picture, so that the glass caught the spectrum and you could just see a little bit of light hitting the cut-glass, like a rainbow catching the letters. It was 1976 and this was before Apple Macs and Photoshop were invented, so we had to do it for real. It was a symbolic idea.

Unfortunately one of the head men at Conde Nast Europe had
other ideas and wanted to see the repeat of a red cover
that had been very successful for French "Vogue". It is
magazine folklore, that if you have a red cover you get
better sales. We had to re-shoot the glass, this time with
a red background, but the subtlety of the idea was lost and
the spectrum was eliminated by the background colour. That
was the day I decided to move on, although it would be
another year before I finally left.

Equally, it's sales folklore that green doesn't sell. I've
always liked taking chances on covers. But sometimes you
have to fight for them. The Green Jelly cover was never
intended as a cover shot either. It was a picture made by
Willy Christie and fashion editor, Grace Coddington. I
wanted it as a cover. Grace and I went to the new publishers of "Vogue" to get approval for it, and they gave it the
go-ahead. But the same director who had blocked my
"Crystal" cover got wind of the idea and tried, literally,
to stop the presses in the middle of the print run. But it
was too late. I got the green cover I wanted and confounded
the sceptics: the issue was a great commercial success!

Often the best cover shot has come from the first or last
frame. It's where the unexpected happens. Like the David
Bailey shot of Jackie Bisset which was the last of a session in which every picture had her smiling unconvincingly.
That exposure captured her true feelings as she gritted her
teeth, snarling at Bailey.

Plate-glass photographed for the Diamond Jubilee cover of British Vogue, without the colour background 1976

# VOGUE

British Vogue cover February 1977 ph.Willie Cristie    Lisa Stansfield i-D No.66 February 1989 ph. Phil Inkelbergh

FEB
60p

the fresh taste
of spring

racing green
how to wear it
and what
to wear with what
prettiest new
make–up
colours
tops and tunics
with more dash than cash
springboard to
health
new diets, new exercises,
new you
who's reading what?
the bedside reading guide

# i·D ™

Ozone-friendly!

get earthy!

5 013071 000461

high street fashion    pagan rites and earth magic    raw hide fashion

lisa stansfield    asidi    fresh green UK fashion    recycled artists

THE FUN & GAMES ISSUE    NO.144

cover star: **pj harvey** photographed by **craig mcdean** september 199

£2.20   $5.50

09

9 770262 357020

FRANCS 38 LIRE 9,000 DM 13,50 PESETAS 625 D KR

i-D

©

i-DEAS, FASHION, CLUBS, MUSIC, PE

# WONDER WOMAN!

## POLLY PULLS IT OFF

ARE DRUGS AND VIOLENCE KILLING FOOTBALL?

KIDS IN AMERICA: FROM ROCKERS TO RAVERS

BEHAVING BADLY: BRITAIN'S TEEN HACKERS

JUNGLE HITS JAPAN • SERIOUSLY SEXY FASHION

# VOGUE

MAR 1
35p

special issue
international
fashion

the prettiest
girls
in London,
Rome,
Paris,
Milan,
New York,
Madrid
the clothes
they wear,
the lives
they lead…
plus
Bianca Jagger
a style of her own
Paris collections
colour

# VOGUE

JULY
35p

MIDSUMMER
FASHION
AND BEAUTY
REPORT

best clothes

newest
ideas

sun living
from here to
Mexico,
California
and
Barbados

beauty secrets
from the
sun people

# VOGUE

SEPT 15
40p

Beauty now—
it's enough
to make
you blush…

The new poets
by Derek Mahon…

Dressed to kill—
all-star cast
on the
Orient Express,
photographed
by Snowdon

the looks to put your money on · 40 pages from the new British Ready-to-Wea
· the coat you're looking for · new suit variations ·
the knitting to count on · day and evening dresses, new softness, new shine

i-D MAGAZINE    i-DEAS, FASHION, CLUBS, MUSIC, PEOPLE    NO. 82 JULY 1990  £1.80

THE ANARCHY ISSUE

Adamski + hallot kite.fluinn + F.7.pp Precop + Brian 'Script' Vurna

**Festivals
and raves**
two generations of

**Inspiral
Carpets**
hippies join hands

**life's riot!**

Anarchists – in the poll tax front line ● Anarchic chic ●
Office sabotage – how to get your own back ● The other
side of Eastern Europe – punks, skateboards and acid
house ● The house sound of Sheffield ●

USA $4.95    07

9 770262 357006

FRANCS 33 LIRE 5.960 DM 12 PESETAS M5.D KR 41

THE TALENT ISSUE

i-DEAS, FASHION, CLUBS, MUSIC, PEOPLE

125 february 1994  cover star justine frischman, elastica

**ICE CUBE
GEORGE CLINTON
MANIC STREET PREACHERS
ELASTICA · TRASH GLAMOUR
MOOD DRUGS & HAPPY PILLS**

# UP! UP! UP!
## THE RISING STARS OF '94

£1.95  $

9 770262 357013    02

FRANCS 35 LIRE 7,100 DM 13.00 PESETAS 5H5

VOGUE
Gioiello

SPLASH!

smeraldi, oro, argento, coralli, perle e turchesi

OROLOGI
waterproof e preziosi

ATTUALITA'
argenti veneziani del '700
antichi ori celtici
gioielli messicani e peruviani

top: British Vogue 1981 ph. Bailey   Italian Vogue 1974 ph. Bailey   Italian Vogue 1972 ph. Bailey   British Vogue 1981 ph. Fabrizio Ferri   Italian Vogue ph. Toscani

VOGUE

SEPT 1
50p

who's
who

New York's
new supermodel,
Margaux
Hemingway

17

i-D

NO. 90 MARCH 1991 £1.80

i-D MAGAZINE
i-DEAS, FASHION, CLUBS, MUSIC, PEOPLE

LOVE
life!

kylie minogue
on love, life
and manipulation

fetish holidays,
lover's fashion and
the dating game

hard workwear
liverpool's new merseybeat
dance dissident gary clail
feminist porn

03

USA $5.50

9 770262 357006

FRANCE 22 LIRE 5,500 DM 12.50 PESETAS 605 O KR 65

VOGUE

JAN
40p

shameless
escape
from all this
to all that

travel '75
from here to
australia
best holiday
buys from
£50–£5000

'75
from now
to summer
new looks in fashion
make-up,
accessories

health '75
new exercise/diet
keep-fit plan

vogue talent

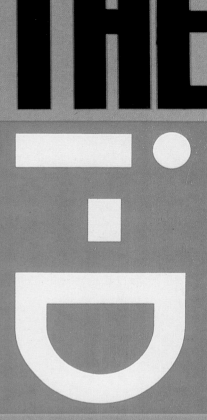

# THE i-D BIBLE

EVERY
ULTI-
MATE
VICTIM'S
HANDBOO

5 013071 000348

i-D MAGAZINE No. 33 FEBRUARY 1986 £1.00

# i-D

## THE COOL ISSUE

+

ool out sister!
ivienne Westwood
aul Rutherford
ashion survival guide

CHILL OUT

Plus music, fashion, style + soho cool

THE INDISPENSABLE DOCUMENT OF FASHION STYLE AND IDEAS

19

i·D

Richard 'Hardware' Stanley + Soh? + the new modernists

**super
nature**

**The Happy
Mondays in Ibiza**

**Thailand —
party paradise**

USA $4.95

*Postponing death — can we live to 150?* ● *NLP — the power of
persuasion* ● *The green movement — too successful for its
own good?* ● *New British black comedy* ● *Positively pertinent
fashion* ● *Fashion: black is back*

FRANCS 31 LIRE 5.900 DM 12 PESETAS 665 D KR 49

# WORLDWIDE MANUAL OF STYLE

THE RED-HOT ISSUE

MAY 1985 £1.00

# i-D

INDISPENSABLE DOCUMENT
SHION, STYLE & IDEAS

5 013071 000034

THE SURVIVAL ISSUE    NO.149

cover star: **kate moss**

# i-D

i-DEAS, FASHION, CLUBS, MUSIC, PEOPLE

£2.20   $5.75

**KATE MOSS**

**JARVIS COCKER**

**PRINCE NASEEM**

**IRVINE WELSH**

**NICK CAVE**

**LOU REED**

**LL COOL J**

**LOUISE WENER**

**EWAN MCGREGOR**

9 770262 357020

02

FRANCS 38 LIRE 8.000 DM 13.50 PES 675 PESETAS PKG 07.95

THE SMART ISSUE

i·D

i-DEAS, FASHION, CLUBS, MUSIC, PEOPLE

123 december 1993   i·D   cover star: kate moss

# LOVE IT!

## KATE MOSS TELLS ALL

## SNOOP DOGGY DOGG
## MALCOLM McLAREN •PULP
## HELMUT LANG •TIM ROTH
## THE RETURN OF THE SUIT

£1.95   $4.95

9 770262 357013

FRANCS 35 LIRE 7.100 DM 13.00 PESETAS 595 D KR 53

# VOGUE

## it's all British

**50 pages of best buys from top to toe**

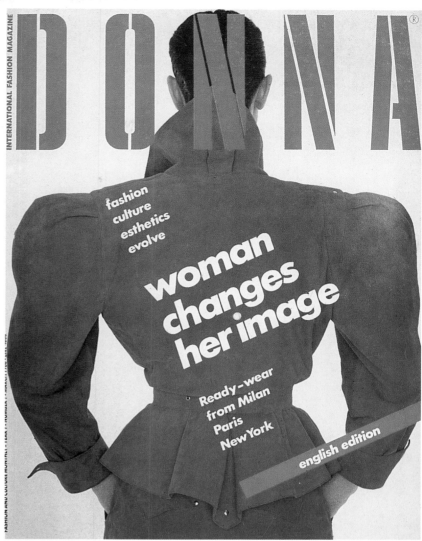

# DOSNA

fashion
culture
esthetics
evolve

## woman changes her image

Ready - wear
from Milan
Paris
New York

*english edition*

# i-D

## positive power!
### beef it up!

*kills all known germs dead*

**Asian power Tokyo power Paris power Black power Religious power Metal power**

5 013071 000485

# i-D

i-DEAS, FASHION, CLUBS, MUSIC, PEOPLE

**Primal Scream**
get loaded with Irvine Welsh

**Christy Turlington**
confessions of a supermodel

**Jungle!**
the last dance underground

## the truth about
## drugs

the highs and lows of drug culture

£1.95   $4.95

9 770262 357013   05

**Plus...** Get wired with our new cybertech section!
Glamorous new school sportswear ● Tales from the psychedelic front

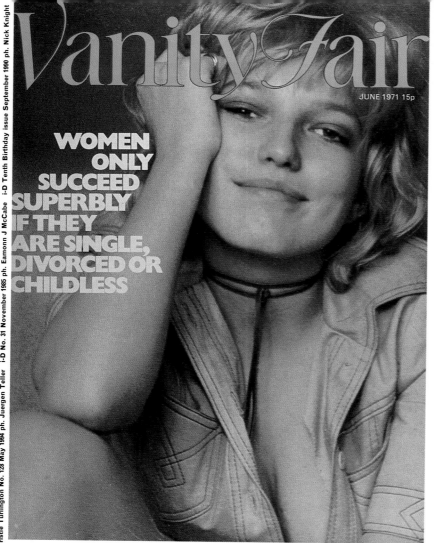

top: First Vogue cover using a Polaroid x 70 No. 128 March 1994 ph. Nick Knight

bottom: Charlotte i-D No. 68 April 1988 ph.Nick Knight   Christie Turlington No. 128 May 1994 ph. Juergen Teller   i-D No. 31 November 1985 ph. Eamonn J McCabe   i-D Tenth Birthday issue September 1990 ph. Nick Knight   Donna No. 68 March 1989 ph. Toscani   Vanity Fair June 1971 ph. Frank Horvat   British Vogue Getaway May 1974 ph. Bailey, a front projection

**Vanity Fair**

JUNE 1971 15p

WOMEN ONLY SUCCEED SUPERBLY IF THEY ARE SINGLE, DIVORCED OR CHILDLESS

**VOGUE**

MAY 35p

GETAWAY

Get up and go holiday fashion All-change sunshine beauty plus Vogue Living and Men in Vogue spring/summer report

WOMAN IN STYLE

the spectator issue

i-D MAGAZINE No. 31 NOVEMBER 1985 £1.00

**i-D**

the indispensable document of fashion style & ideas

ONE EYED

MONSTER!

NEX SEASON OF ENTERTAINMENT......WITH LOTS OF SPUNKY BITS!!

5 013071 000096

10TH BIRTHDAY SPECIAL   NO.84 SEPTEMBER 1990  £1.80

**i-D**

30 PAGES OF STREET FASHION

**10 UP**

THE i-D FORUMS LOOKING INTO THE FUTURE OF FASHION MUSIC DESIGN FILMS BOOKS

USA $4.05

09

9 770262 357006

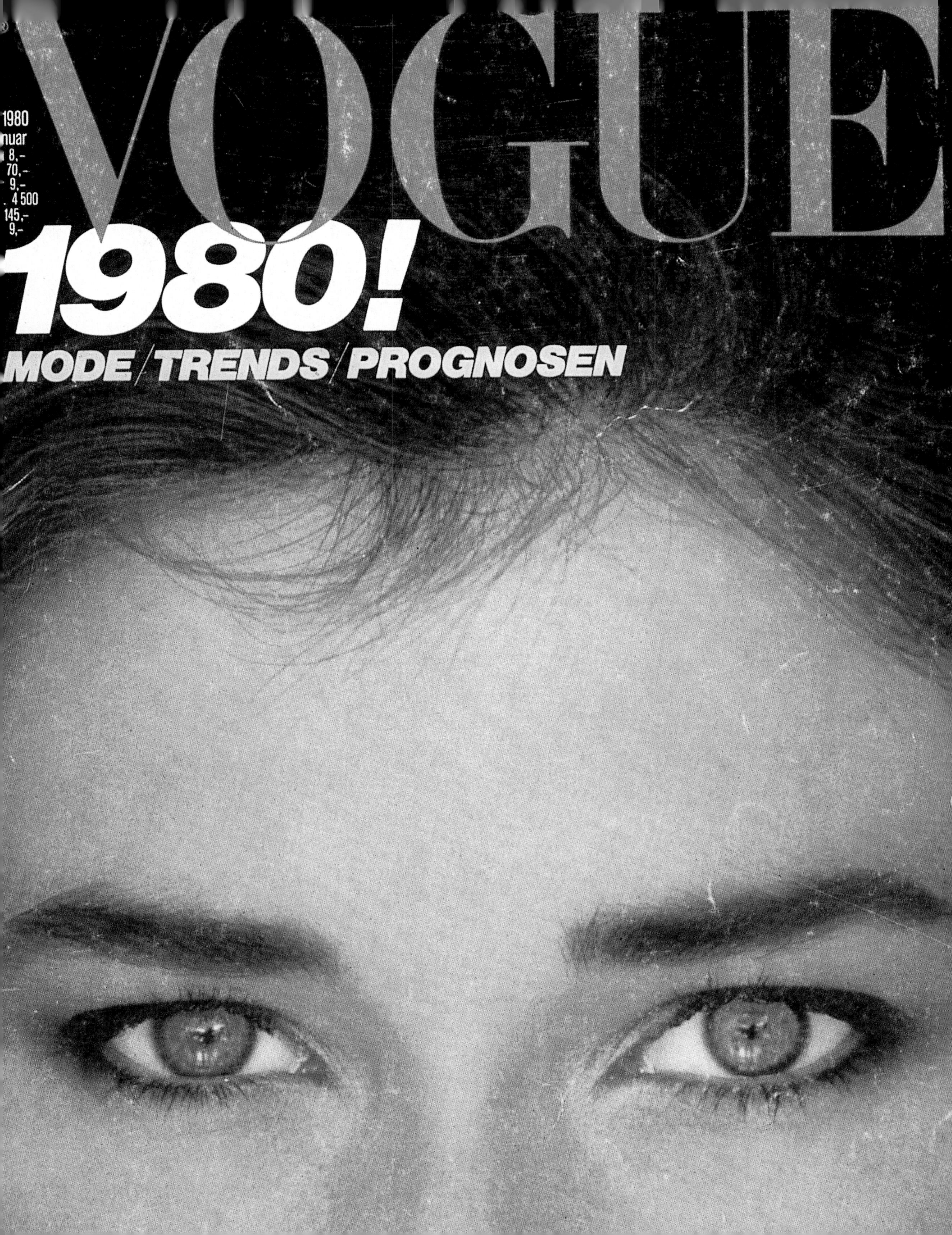

# VOGUE

1980
nuar
8,–
70,–
9,–
. 4 500
145,–
9,–

## 1980!
### MODE / TRENDS / PROGNOSEN

# i-D

©

i-DEAS, FASHION, CLUBS, MUSIC, PEOPLE

# unzip!

## THE UNDRESSED ISSUE
# DO WE HAVE TO SPELL IT OUT?

£2.20 US$5.75

9 770262 357020

12

CAN $6.95 FRANCS 38 LIRE 9,000 DM 13.50 PESETAS 625 D KR 50

British Vogue June 1977 ph. Barry Lategan    unused cover for British Vogue March 1977 ph. Fouli Elia

There's a story behind the Dior cover. One of the last covers that I did before leaving "Vogue" was a Barry Lategan beauty session with a stunning hood hiding the girl's eyes. We convinced the distribution manager that this cover would be successful - the make-up credit went to Revlon who paid for the gatefold so that we could run the image landscape. Dior, who booked more advertising pages through the year, wanted the following issue to be equally strong - with their own make-up credit. Fouli Elia, the photographer, was given the task of photographing a fuscia pink dress and when I went down to the studio the two of us agreed the result was going to look dull. I'd tried for some time to convince the management to allow a nipple on the cover, so I asked the model if she had any objections to a paparazzi-style picture which captured her getting changed in the dressing room. The result showed her clutching the dress, not wearing it - nipple exposed. The model's famously "dazzling" smile was eclipsed by the twinkle in her eye. I prepared a presentation of the cover with a print.

It was a Friday afternoon and the editor at "Vogue", Bea Miller, and I convinced the distribution manager that this was a good follow up to the Lips and Hood cover, and when I went home for the weekend I assumed it had been sent off to the printer. Monday morning and there's something going on. My art department felt like a morgue. Nobody was saying anything. But I soon learnt that the cover was being re-shot and that I was banned from talking to Fouli at the studio! It was a dull exit from "Vogue" but over all I look

back and think how many brilliant opportunities the five years had provided. Working with people of such high calibre was an amazing education. Twenty years on Matt, my son, shot the cover of the Undressed issue of "i-D" with a top young New York model Jaime Rishar. Inside we showed the image which the newsagents still say is unacceptable - the picture of Jaime flashing her nipple!

After "Vogue" there was the opportunity to do something new. "Donna" was launched by an ex-editorial director of "L'Uomo Vogue", Flavio Lucini. It was intended to look at fashion from a different perspective. I devised the graphics so that I could design it from London. Everything was set in one typeface, Futura, in ten point on a fixed measure and just enlarged up and down so that the design was really minimal. The photography wasn't brilliant, so I used to bang the type over the pictures and it was a bit of a shock for the advertisers. The graphics were strong but within two issues they were watering it down.

I'd been promised the opportunity to produce a magazine on street-style, but Flavio said," no one's interested but we'll wait six months and see." Then he started a menswear magazine and I got fed up waiting. So I started trying to find a publisher in Italy for my idea. I went to this guy called Jolly who had a company called Better Badges and was the main printer of fanzines in London. I said I wanted to do a fashion fanzine. He said," OK the deal is if I print them you buy copies off me. We'll do 2000 to begin with and distribute them through record shops."

# i-D

STARRING:
CAPRICORN
AQUARIUS
PISCES
ARIES
TAURUS
GEMINI
CANCER
LEO
VIRGO
LIBRA
SCORPIO
SAGITTARIUS

★ ALLSTAR ★

the health & efficiency issue

i-D MAGAZINE No. 29 SEPTEMBER 1985 £1.00

# i-D

the indispensable document
of fashion style & ideas

CROP TO FIT!

5 013071 000072

in the pink with a picture of health!

THE HAPPY ISSUE

i-D MAGAZINE NO 54 DECEMBER 1987/JANUARY 1988 £1.50/$4.50

# i-D

"trendy fashion magazine"

5 013071 000331

GET UP! GET HAPPY!

THE VISIONARY ISSUE    NO.133    cover stars: **brett anderson** and **stella tennant**  photographed by jean baptiste mondino OCTOBER

£2.20 $5.

9 770262 357020

FRANCS 39 LIRE 10.000 GM 13.50 PESETAS

i-DEAS, FASHION, CLUBS, MUSIC, PEOPLE

FASHION'S
FRESH
VISION

quentin tarantino
luscious jackson
liza bruce
steve albini
billion dollar babewear
art terrorism
jungle chic
the new mods

## suede
### The Art Of Falling Apart

i-D covers No. 14 ph. Nick Knight   No. 29 September 1985 ph. Nick Knight   Two covers i-D Japan ph. Takashi Homma   i-D Smiley by Steve Male ph. Jean Baptiste Mondino   Brett Anderson and Stella Tennant i-D October 1994 ph. Jean Baptiste Mondino   Björk + Goldie No. 154 July 1996 ph. Lorenzo Agius

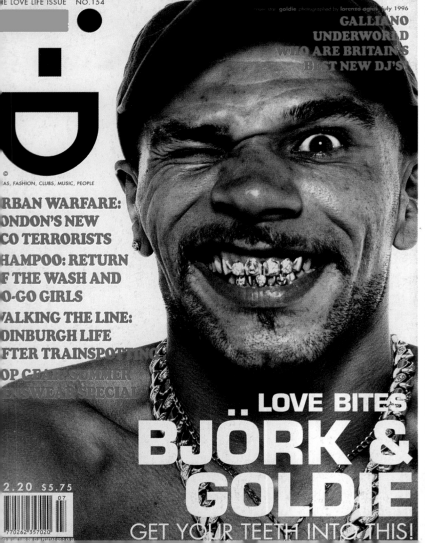

# i·D

POWER
CRIME
SPORT
ETCET
CETC...
PLUS+

# WULI DANCING

32

"i-D" covers started out as a pure graphic. The logo is a graphic icon for a winking eye and smiling face. From issue five, the month that Lady Di became a princess, I produced "i-D"'s first winking cover with her face - the D-I-Y issue! Since then, every person who has appeared on the cover of "i-D" has had to make an attempt - with mixed success - to wink and duplicate what has become the "i-D" trademark. The problem has been that many wannabe cover stars have spent hours practising in front of the mirror to perfect their wink - unfortunately they practise with the wrong eye. It's left eye open, right eye closed - but in the mirror they see the logo in reverse.

The wink cover was intended to prompt an interaction and collaboration necessary between photographer and cover-star. It is an added "problem" - something that has to be solved, making the solution more interesting. Each cover is a challenge that has been solved continually and different-ly. I've always believed that if you gave a dozen photogra-phers the same camera and the same subject you would get a dozen different interpretations. This has been proved by the diversity of "i-D" covers. This restriction has made us unique. The solid requirement of reinforcing the logo on the cover sets "i-D" apart from the sameness of all other titles. As we head towards issue 200, new models and top photographers - who began their careers with "i-D" - are still contributing to the "i-D" cover solution.

Nick Knight, photographer: "That 'i-D' wink, which Terry insists on for the cover shot, has been the bane of my

life...the number of really pretty girls who turn into gar-goyles because they can't wink."

Producing "i-D" in the days before computer graphics I used silk screen techniques which produced block colouring, and fluorescent inks for optical colour contrasts. Artwork was cut by hand from photocopies and bromide prints. The early issues were bog-standard A4 sheets stapled landscape. The long suffering repro house, Latent Image, made our first full-colour separation for the back cover of issue 2. When Thomas Degan and I went to collect copies of the first issue from Better Badges in Portobello Road, we saw this girl whose job it was to punch the staples into fanzines. She was called Scrubber, and had actually had the morning off to appear in court charged with grievous bodily harm, but we thought she looked great with this big smile on her face. Thomas took her picture and she became our first full colour portrait.

Omaid Hiwaizi, ex-"i-D" art editor: "When we needed to reconstruct the 'i-D' logo for the Mac, it was amazing to see the hand drawn original. There were loads of 'lay-lines' in the logo and Terry tried to pretend to me that he hadn't added them afterwards. But, either way, there is a mystical correctness in the logo because when certain points of the star are joined up they dissect the dot of the 'i'."

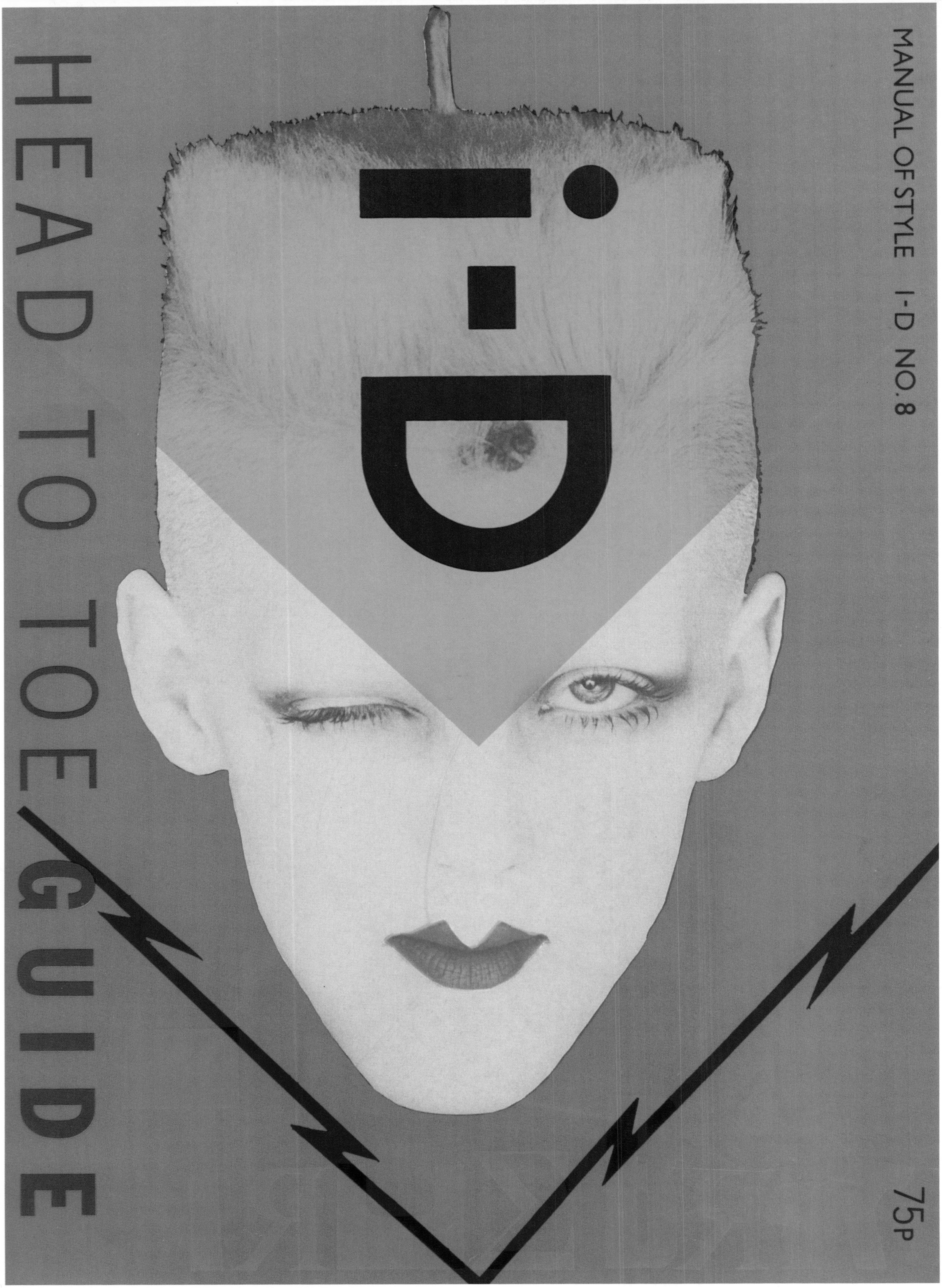

HEAD TO TOE GUIDE

i-D

MANUAL OF STYLE  I-D NO.8

75P

towards

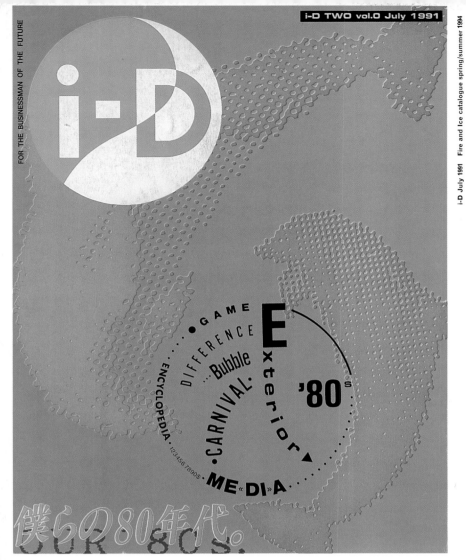

i-D

●GAME

DIFFERENCE

ENCYCLOPEDIA

..Bubble

E

CARNIVAL.

·1234567890$

Exterior▶

ME«DI»A

'80s

僕らの80年代。

OUR 80s.

i-D July 1991   Fire and Ice catalogue spring/summer 1994

34

Collaborating with the repro house Latent Image has been an
ongoing technical education. The early apprentices, who got
used to our multiple layered artworks, now operate the most
sophisticated electronic page make-up systems available.
Peter Rodgers and Colin Fitzgerald's patience has tolerated
masses of experimentation. With my art editors, Alex
McDowell, Moira Bogue, Robin Derrick, Steve Male, Neil
Edwards, Omaid Hiwaizi, Scott King and most recently
Brendan Parker, we explored the art of illegibility,
tongue-in-cheek graphics and classic, modern typography.
Classic graphic formats have always interested me.
At "Vogue" I was often accused of not treating the photographic subject seriously but I believe that irreverence is
healthy. When Dennis Morris, my partner at the time, photographed John Lydon and his new band PIL, we put a teardrop of glycerine in his eye - a pastiche of a 'L'Uomo
Vogue cover. I don't believe in taking anything too seriously, and nothing is sacred.

the sea

FIRE & ICE

# PUBLIC IMAGE

*first issue*

RELIGION
## ATTACK

**public image**
## THEME
*Annalisa*

album sleeve for Public Image Limited ph. Dennis Morris    i-D cover March 1985 ph. Eamonn J McCabe

WORLDWIDE MANUAL OF STYLE

MARCH 1985    £1.00

THE i-SPY ISSUE

i-D

THE INDISPENSABLE DOCUMENT
OF FASHION, STYLE & IDEAS.

lues!

spies+lies

INVESTIGATE! INITIATE!

5 013071 000010

i-D MAGAZINE No.23

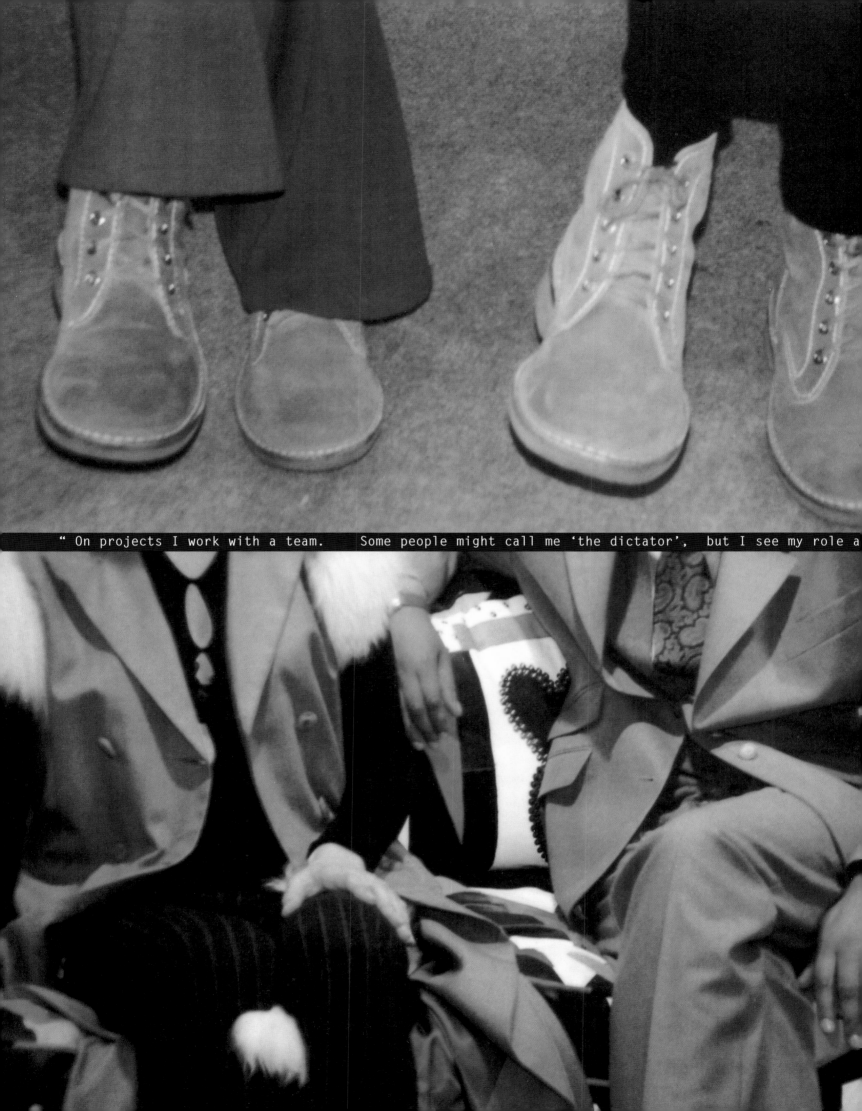

" On projects I work with a team.   Some people might call me 'the dictator',   but I see my role a

a catalyst!"

Spread from British Vogue October 1974 · Vogue cover October 1974 · both ph. Toscani

VOGUE'S BEST BUYS

SHEER GLITTER

Sequins and silver for sparkle, the coat for rainshine . . . Dress of sequins and wool/acrylic, above: golden/black/bronze vest over long jetshine skirt by Neil & Laura Phillips, about £78, at Dickins & Jones; Cavendish House, Cheltenham; Pixies Place, Pershore. Sequinned jacket, £32, at Biba. Necklace by Gay Designs. Sequinned bandeau, Juliet Dunn. Lurex tights, Mary Quant. Silvery shoes, Dorothée Bis, about £36, to order at Elle, Bond St. Silvery grey Ban-Lon jersey, top right, silvery lace crossed with stripes of silvery sequins. Anne Tyrrell at John Marks, £36.95, at Harrods. Solitaire, Brighton; Fenwick, Newcastle. Diamanté tiaras, £1.80 each, at Biba. Palest tights, Pretty Polly. Shoes, as above. The coat for shining rainy evenings, centre right, silvery coated nylon with grey Borg roll collar, buttoned down the left side. £27.10. Silver and gold diamond panelled clutch bag, about £9. Both at Biba. Lurex tights, silvery shoes, as above. Man's velvet dinner suit, jacket with silk lapels,

£85, satin-stripe dress shirt, £12.50, socks, 99p, Cecil Gee, New Bond St. Velvet bow tie, £3, Turnbull & Asser. Black patent shoes, £18.50, Russell & Bromley. Orrefors champagne glass, £1.41 each, at Liberty. Shimmying dress of black, golden and silver sequins, right, with deep V'd neck and dipped hemline. £47.50. Diamanté necklace, £2.95. Both at Biba. Diamanté earrings, Ken Lane. Black/silver Lurex tights, Mary Quant. Silver shoes with high shaped heel, pointed toe, Dorothée Bis, about £36 to order, at Elle, Bond Street. Stuart Crystal champagne glass, £8.60 each, Liberty. Champagne, throughout, by Moet & Chandon, from Nichols Bar at the Café Royal. Hair by Pat at Vidal Sassoon. Shops, sizes, colours, see Stockists

183

40

"On projects I work with a team. Some people might call me 'the dictator', but I see my role as a catalyst!"

I choose the people I collaborate with when the feeling seems right. Working with people to form mutual respect that's what I like, with each person having their own creative role. At the point when a working partnership becomes a hassle, something that generates a negative rather than a positive energy, that's time to quit. It's so much better to work in an environment where the process of collaboration and creativity feels rewarding.

Toscani was always a maverick but working as a team I was very happy with the results we got. We met in 1971, introduced by the menswear editor at "Vanity Fair", Erica Chrome. When I was art director of "Vanity Fair", which was published by the National Magazine Company, Conde Nast had all the world-class photographers under contract; Irving Penn, Guy Bourdin, Helmut Newton, Bailey and Clive Arrowsmith. So they couldn't work for any rival publisher. I had to find a new bunch of photographers which could compete with the manicured image of "Vogue". Where American "Vogue"'s style, with Richard Avedon's cover portraits was hard edged, I wanted more flesh and blood, more soul and more energy. I went for the realism of documentary photography, working with people like Frank Horvat (the Cartier-Bresson of fashion photography), David Montgommery, Saul Leiter and Peter Knapp. Oliviero Toscani was part of a new European bunch I started using which included Hans Feurer,

Arthur Elgort, Uli Rose and Richard Avedon's ex-assistant Alex Chatelain.

I never studied the history of photography or the history of art direction, but by working with an international group of photographers I would hear about other magazine art directors like Ruth Ansel at "Harpers Bazaar", Peter Knapp at "ELLE" in Paris, Alex Lieberman at American "Vogue" and Barney Wan at British "Vogue". After "Vanity Fair" folded, I was returning pictures to Paris-based photographers by hand. I met up with Peter Knapp in his studio and he congratulated me on landing the position of art editor at British "Vogue" as the art director Barney Wan was leaving. I hadn't even had an interview, so it was the first I'd heard about it. Peter told me to call and after three lunches I was installed at Vogue House. For six months I wondered what I was doing there.

When I first worked at "Vogue" it was standard practice to retouch every flaw on a photograph. I'd never before enjoyed that questionable luxury, to redraw or re-shape to such an extent. Because the photo lab was just one floor above I would spend hours seeing that the quality of a print was what each photographer wanted. But retouching the creases out of a model's trouser leg seemed to kill an image, rather than give it life. At "Vogue" there were three full-time retouchers and we'd sometimes joke that it might save time and money if the photo had been taken with cardboard tubes shoved up the models' trouser legs, so as to control the natural folds of the fabric!

# VOGUE

40p
OCT 1

picture
yourself
like
this...

evening
fashion
and
beauty

40
pages

LOOKS IN THE STARLIGHT NOW

## Monday, early am...

Woken by strange crunching noise. Put celery on shopping
list and leant out window to water geraniums.
Getting another angle on things — flyover looked quite odd.
Not me, though, in my new flowered cream satin kimono
and some café au lait lace and satin from my favourite
underclothes people. N.B. Get eyes tested.

*Kimono, £11, from Aurium. Bra, knickers, suspender
belt, by Janet Reger, from a range at Fenwick. Sheer
cream stockings by Pretty Polly. Pink maribou mules,
£18.95, from Rayne.*

### Later, am...

Stairs not there, so took short cut
to town, helped by streamlined
denim jumpsuit.
That's me in the next picture, too,
waving for a plane.
Couldn't make it without a hitch...

*Jumpsuit, zipped, by Experience
Clothing Company, £22, at
Experience, 26 Duke St, W.1.
Red and blue shoulder purses,
by Jap, £8.95, each at Jap and
Joseph. White heart earrings,
Emeline. White sun specs, £2,
Bombacha. Red/white spotted
cotton kerchief, Herbert
Johnson. Big blue watch by
Gay Design. Shops, sizes,
colours, see Stockists.*

124
125

British Vogue December 1975, in the year of the disaster movie ph. Toscani

42

Toscani and I continued to work together after I left
"Vogue" in 1977. He was indirectly responsible for my leaving. He'd been asked to contribute to a book called
"Masters of Erotic Photography". He told the publishers
that they didn't need photographers, they needed an art
director, and hooked me up with Tim Chadwick and Michael
Haggiag who had just founded Aurum Press. He also introduced me to the publisher of "Sportswear International", to
art direct their pilot issue. Toscani inspired me to work
like a paratrooper: small bag, big ideas! Travelling Europe
became a regular occurrence. When the kids were on holiday
from school we combined work with pleasure and often ended-
up staying at Toscani's beautiful home in Tuscany.
Tricia Jones: "Terry is the man I love and the man I've
been married to for nearly thirty years. He's a man of many
contrasts: an inspirational teacher, but also a hard
taskmaster who can be an impossible ball breaker! He is a
perfectionist who will make untold work for himself trying
to constantly improve something, but then has the ability
to live with whatever decision was right on that day and
that deadline. He is a dictator who thinks he believes in
democracy, and an influential communicator who becomes
incoherent with his instructions when he's really busy.
He's a whole host of contradictions: the tallest short man,
the untidiest Virgo. He lacks any personal vanity (much to
my despair), yet is the owner and inspiration behind one of
the most influential style magazines. He is a lateral
thinker but impossibly obstinate, and for every person in
whom he commands absolute loyalty and respect there is
probably another whom he drives to distraction!"
For Tricia's fiftieth birthday, a small group of friends
gathered in our kitchen where "i-D" got laid out over
seven-teen years ago. Several of the original editors who
began their careers somewhere between the studio at the
top of my house and late-night spaghetti suppers have
stayed close friends.
My aim is to work as a catalyst. At my first job in a
design studio, with Ivan Dodd, I learnt that a catalyst
connects things together. Making connections is part of
the creative process. I try to capture an image with life
- graphically. To capture that moment is to get a result.
Tricia, my wife, has been my most important collaborator.
I remember the exact moment we made eye contact and met.
We were students, and it was at a Georgie Fame gig at the
University Hall in Bristol. She has been my major collaborator and critic. Her energy is a force that cannot be
underestimated. Energy is the life force that makes connections move, but the creative director must decide
which direction to go in.

vibes

MAXIMUM EFFECT

"HATS SHOULD BE FUN, FLIRTY, NAUGHTY."

So says STEPHEN JONES, fab hat designer. "People often remark on how sexy my hats are - it seems to just happen that way, I subconsciously make them like that."

On Sex Appeal: "The knowledge that one is sexy kills sex appeal. Trying to be sexy is not sex appeal, especially in men. My own sexiest parts are my elbows."

See the current Stephen Jones hat collection at 34 Lexington St - contact Sybylle on (01) 734 9666. Watch out for the new Winter Collection showing at the above office, soon to be available from Harrods, Browns, Mirror Mirror in Dublin, Daisy in Germany and Bloomingdales in the USA.

1234567890

Photos Toscani

FAB PETER, decked head to shin in Leigh Bowery gear. Boots from Vivienne Westwood Worlds End.

FOR BRIGHTLY COLOURED FACES, CHECK OUT:
Stargazer stall, Great Gear Market Kings Rd for fluorescent waterbased eye shadows, £2.99; fluorescent nail varnish, £1.50; fluorescent hair gel, 99p.
Liberated Lady, 408 Kings Rd for fluorescent hair spray, £2.25; glitter gel for face and body, £1.50.
FOR THAT SPECIAL LIFT: check out Marley's at the Great Gear Market for platform boots of all sizes in snakeskin and plain

JEWELLERY CHECK-OUTS:
Antonia Lesley for unusual designs of clustered gems at NoYes Floral St, Michael Frey in South Molton St and Roxy in Kensington Church St.
Brand Spanking for large fluorescent eye-catching designs, available from Hyper Hyper.
Jack Brenden's for a good selection of studs, badges, bootlaces, tie pins and other Ted, Rocker, Punk and Mod adornments, in Richmond Rd Kingston.

MINIMAL IMPACT

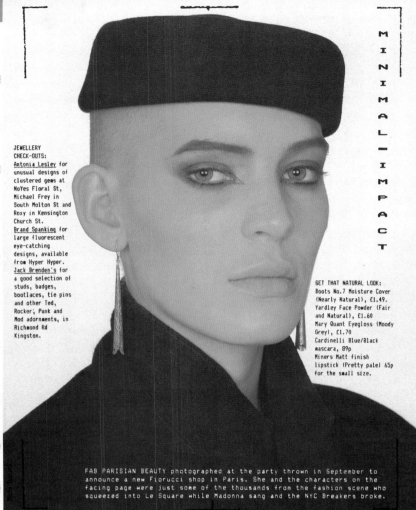

GET THAT NATURAL LOOK:
Boots No.7 Moisture Cover (Nearly Natural), £1.49.
Yardley Face Powder (Fair and Natural), £1.60
Mary Quant Eyegloss (Moody Grey), £1.70
Cardinelli Blue/Black mascara, 89p.
Miners Matt finish lipstick (Pretty pale) 65p for the small size.

FAB PARISIAN BEAUTY photographed at the party thrown in September to announce a new Fiorucci shop in Paris. She and the characters on the facing page were just some of the thousands from the fashion scene who squeezed into Le Square while Madonna sang and the NYC Breakers broke.

17

Die neue Schlichtheit entbehrt durchaus nicht der kleinen Raffinessen. Da gibt es sehr listige Farbkompositionen, sehr ausgefeilte geometrische Figuren. Die Zeit ist ganz offensichtlich vorbei, in der die Rocklänge diktierte, was Mode ist.

EINFACH MIT FINESSE

Rechts: Grüner Rock aus Baumwollsatin. Dazu gestricktes Jerseyhemd in Graphit und weißer Baumwollblazer mit kurzem Arm. Modell: Issey Miyake.

Links: Mittelding zwischen Hosenkleid und Jumpsuit, in Grün. Im Rückenteil zwei aufgesetzte Taschen. Dazu eine grüne und schwarze Wendejacke im Judoschnitt. Modell: Jean-Paul Gaultier.

76
77

FIORUCCI

SPRING/SUMMER '85 COLLECTION

BEACH AND TOWN

HOLD YO

SUZY SPIDER SCARVES

HOT LIPS & RED ACCESSORIES

Fiorucci catalogues    bottom: winter 1984 ph. Toscani    top: summer 1985 ph. Roberto Carra

FIORUCCI

BE FABULOUS

FIORUCCI AUTUMN/WINTER 1984

AARGH!

MY WAY SEE-THROUGH BAGS

BRIGHTEN UP THE SWEAT WITH PRINT

HORSES

BIG, BAG AND BEAUTIFUL

<#>

AUDACE: coraggioso; oltraggioso; spregiudicato

BE DARING

PHOTOGRAPHED BY NICK KNIGHT

STYLING BY SIMON FOXTON

HAIR BY KEVIN RYAN AT ANTENNA
GROOMING BY FRANCES HATHAWAY AT FACES
LOCATION: LIPSTICK STUDIOS LONDON
MODELS: AMANDA KING, DANCER WITH MICHAEL
CLARK, OKE AT NEVS (CURRENTLY DANCING IN
CHESS), STUNT MAN GLEN DAVIS AT NEVS, WILL
JUMP OUT OF A WINDOW IF YOU WANT, DAVID
WEARING, DANCER, SPOTTED AT THE FRIDGE
DANCING FOR PROJ-X ●

**SCHOOL'S BACK!**

Boiled beef and carrots, fags behind the bike-sheds and heads down the toilet. Ring! Ring! Yes, school is back again. And come lunchtime the laddies come out to play-act: Flashman, Dennis The Menace and Billy Whizz with not-so-baggy trousers, not-so-dirty shirts . . . but definitely a tap on the head with a plastic cup. With their tongues in their cheeks they pile out for a scrap, a joke and a chase round the playground — all good, clean, healthy fun.

Feast your eyes on the following pages and watch some geezers in real Men's clothing pushing out their chests and reading i-D behind their text books. "Who stole my ruler!"

42

For clothes details refer to page 57

43

i-D No. 37 1986 ph. Nick Knight   i-D No. 40 1986 ph. Nick Knight and Simon Foxton

46

As an art director I always try to place my trust with the photographer. It is their job to capture the spark of life. I like to work with photographers who can capture the energy of the moment. As the director you must anticipate the action, or make it happen. Portrait photography is a collaboration between the subject and the photographer. The photographer I worked with on the Chipie Jeans campaign compared photography to the starter pistol at a speedway race. The racers have to anticipate the moment the gun will be fired just as a photographer must anticipate when to click the shutter. When it is a collaboration, the image is given as a gift by the subject to the photographer, rather than being stolen. That rapport and trust between subject and photographer is vital.

But chance is not a question of luck. We make chances happen. More and more I believe our energy effects chance. I try to work as a mirror, reflecting the strength of other people's talent and involving them in the problem solving by magnifying their skills. My role is like a record producer working with an orchestra and a conductor to create a piece of music, with the photographer playing the role of the conductor. I consider myself more of a director or catalyst than an artist or designer.

I build working relationships and go through long periods collaborating with a few photographers. Collaborations are formed by bouncing ideas around for the style of the photography and layouts. The partnership between an art director and a group of photographers is crucial to any maga-zine. I choose to work with the best photographer I can on the day a job has to be done. The day effects how a job will look as we have no control over weather or time - two factors which are crucial to the result.

Between work trips abroad, I founded "i-D" in August 1980. Toscani, Caroline Baker and I had joked about infiltrating the fashion industry's commercial image three years before. We never had time to write our manifesto, but, somehow over the years of publishing "i-D", 'the school of "i-D"' has invaded the mainstream.

Many people simply walked into the office and were given a pencil. I have absolute belief that everyone has some form of creative talent that should never be wasted and I'm constantly putting people to work!!! After all these years those who survived my irrational way of working have gone on to establish careers in all branches of the media. I see them as the "i-D" mafia.

Nick Knight came to my studio while he was a student at Bournemouth College, and since shooting Sade for a cover back in 1983 has been a major contributor throughout the life of "i-D".

Nick Knight, photographer: "Terry's attitude to photography was against everything I had learnt. He taught me not to be precious, and I know I'm guilty of making things too complicated. When I shot the hundred portraits in the 'i-D' identity parade which appeared in the fifth birthday issue, Terry said," you've got half an hour with each person, two rolls of two and a quarter, that's twenty shots, one five

# i-D

## wise up!

ENSWEAR SPECIAL

OLLY JOHNSON

ARCELONA

HE CHRISTIANS

HICAGO HOUSE MUSIC

★

OGER DACK

RT POP!

ORKERS FOR FREEDOM

APLES FUNK

HE SUN-BED KIDS

school's back

THE EDUCATION ISSUE

5 013071 000188

HE INDISPENSABLE DOCUMENT OF FASHION STYLE AND IDEAS

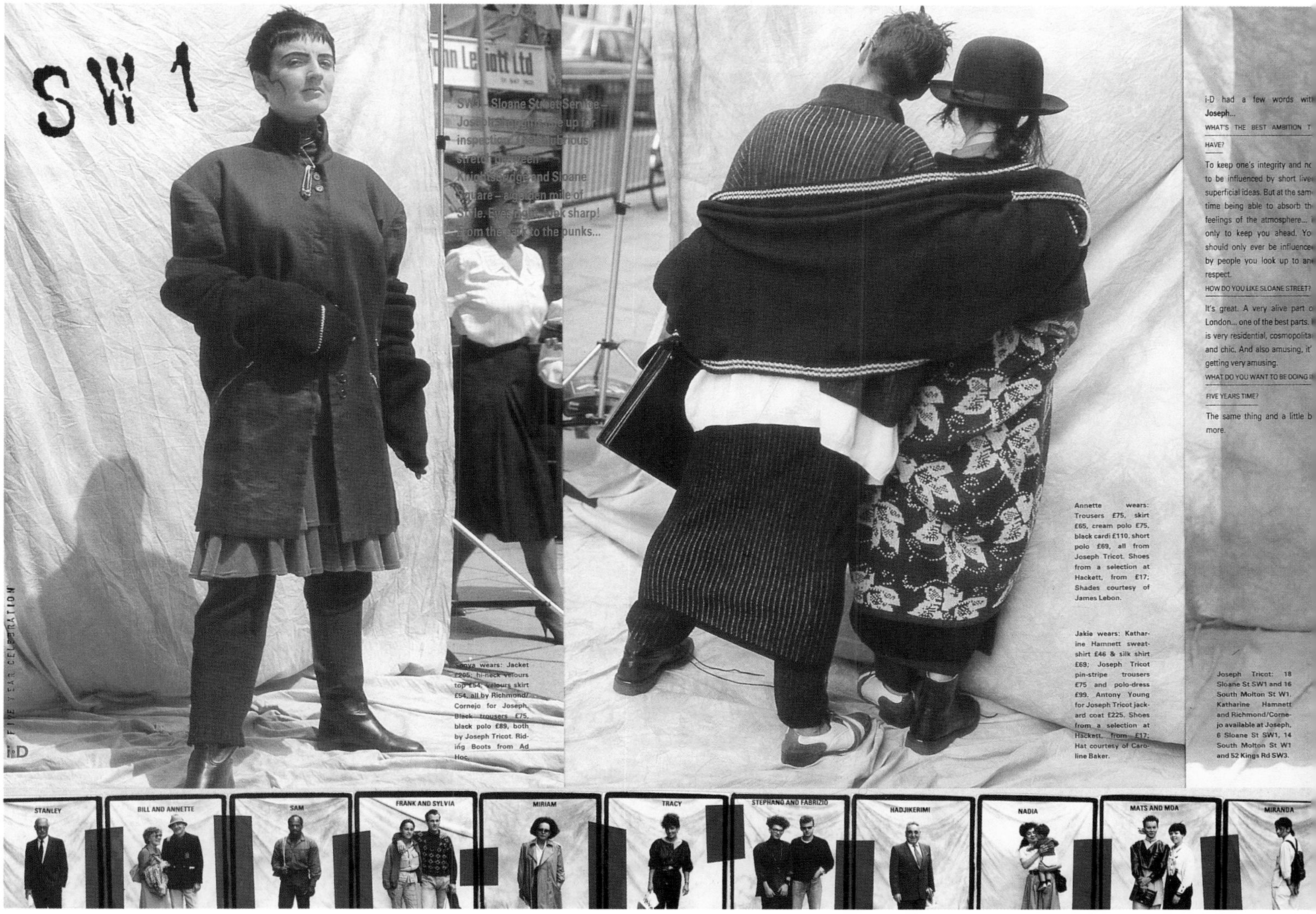

SW 1

SW1 – Sloane Street Service... Joseph [illegible] up for inspection [illegible] Stretch between Knightsbridge and Sloane Square – a [illegible] mile of Style. Even [illegible] look sharp! From the [illegible] to the punks...

[illegible] wears: Jacket £205; hi-neck velours top £54, velours skirt £54, all by Richmond/Cornejo for Joseph. Black trousers £75, black polo £89, both by Joseph Tricot. Riding Boots from Ad Hoc.

Annette wears: Trousers £75, skirt £65, cream polo £75, black cardi £110, short polo £69, all from Joseph Tricot. Shoes from a selection at Hackett, from £17; Shades courtesy of James Lebon.

Jakie wears: Katharine Hamnett sweatshirt £46 & silk shirt £69; Joseph Tricot pin-stripe trousers £75 and polo-dress £99. Antony Young for Joseph Tricot jackard coat £225. Shoes from a selection at Hackett, from £17; Hat courtesy of Caroline Baker.

i-D had a few words with **Joseph...**

WHAT'S THE BEST AMBITION T[O] HAVE?

To keep one's integrity and no[t] to be influenced by short live[d] superficial ideas. But at the sam[e] time being able to absorb th[e] feelings of the atmosphere... [i]... only to keep you ahead. Yo[u] should only ever be influence[d] by people you look up to an[d] respect.

HOW DO YOU LIKE SLOANE STREET?

It's great. A very alive part o[f] London... one of the best parts. [It] is very residential, cosmopolita[n] and chic. And also amusing, it'[s] getting very amusing.

WHAT DO YOU WANT TO BE DOING I[N] FIVE YEARS TIME?

The same thing and a little b[it] more.

Joseph Tricot: 18 Sloane St SW1 and 16 South Molton St W1. Katharine Hamnett and Richmond/Cornejo available at Joseph, 6 Sloane St SW1, 14 South Molton St W1 and 52 Kings Rd SW3.

FIVE YEAR CELEBRATION i-D

STANLEY · BILL AND ANNETTE · SAM · FRANK AND SYLVIA · MIRIAM · TRACY · STEPHANO AND FABRIZIO · HADJIKERIMI · NADIA · MATS AND MOA · MIRANDA

48

Spreads from i-D No. 30 October 1985, special A3 landscape format to celebrate the fifth birthday   top: ph. Eamonn J. McCabe styling Caroline Baker   bottom: ph. Nick Knight, from a series of portraits of 80s faces

**CERITH WYN EVANS** – Film-maker. First appeared in i-D No. 1. Cerith studied at St Martin's School of Art, then the RCA – causing syllabus rumpus wherever he went. Best bit of the 80s: "Falling in love." Most important bit: "Reading 'Les Chants De Maldoror' by Le Comte De Lautreamont." Sum up 1985: "23." What will you be in five years' time?: "A 14 year old Venezuelan prostitute walking the streets of New York." Cerith describes himself as "an artist". Club: Taboo. Record: 'Low Flying Aircraft' – Ann Bean.

**TERRY & TRICIA JONES** – Editor/Art Director/Dog Handler and Extra Pair of Hands/Teacher/Mum. First appeared in i-D No.30. Terry is the man who invented i-D. Trish is now... "A bit fatter, a bit older, but very happy." They both enjoy wild weekends in Wales! Terry says... "The most important event of the 80s? I can only remember what happened yesterday." Club: "My health club"/"Jones & Co when the kids don't quarrel." Record: "I Am A Warrior"/"Feed The World".

**JOHN PEEL** – DJ. First appeared in i-D No. 11. The maverick of pop DJs, forever on the fringe and deliberately only occasionally in vogue. "This year was grossly disfigured by what happened in Brussels. It was hellish, and my vocabulary isn't equal to it. I now understand why my father never talked about the war. But, in the last five years, the most important thing for me has been the birth of two of my children – dull, but true. Five years' time? Playing for Liverpool or doing the same as I am now... I'm a man completely without ambition." Club: Sol Y Sombra. Record: 'Come Back' – Wah! ("The only song of the last five years that I know all the words to.")

**KEANAN** – Fashion Designer. First appeared in i-D No. 16. A student at St Martin's School of Art he is currently recording demos for a record company. "President Reagan has had the most impact recently because of the escalation of the arms race – his commitment to Star Wars is quite frightening. In 1990 I'd like to be making successful records, 'cause I'm a bit of a non-event so far." Club: Primos. Record: 'Anarchy In The UK' – Sex Pistols (Re-release).

**KATE** – Model. First appeared in i-D NO.15. Ex-fab Parisienne beauty now Z Agency corker. She describes herself as "Fairly pleasant." "I've changed a hell of a lot in this decade... changed for the better. 1985 has been an extremely extreme year all round... and in 1990 I hope I'm working in the media." Club: The Wag Club. Record: 'Everything She Wants' – Wham!

**GENESIS P. ORRIDGE** – Pop Singer. First appeare[d] ... Throbbing Gristle, Psychic TV, dry ice, sense of humo[ur] ... "The invention and availability of the black box – capab[le] ... people from drugs without withdrawal symptoms. Mee[t] ... all resulting sexual activities. I'd like to be immensely ric[h] ... deviant behaviour – causing trouble with style. 1985 ha[s] ... when many opportunities were presented to the people ... paranoid. Club: The Palladium. Record: 'Godstar' – Psyc[hic TV]

**MARC ALMOND** – Pop Singer. First appeared in i-D NO.5. Half of Soft Cell, one of The Mambas and cohort to Bronski Jimi. "Everything I've done is important, I wouldn't have got involved if it wasn't. I have changed considerably through I'm still sexy, butch, witty, clever, sensible and vastly talented with a huge penis." Club: "Anything abroad." Record: "Re-issues."

**JAY STRONGMAN** – DJ & Journalist. First appeared in i-D No. 27. One of the handful of crucial London DJs. The 80s?: "The miners' strike. It showed the working class weren't going to toe the line to Thatcherism." Jay the man?: "A bit wiser, less naive." 1990: "I'd like to be living in a socialist Britain." 1985: "The year of change, and also the year that The El-Trains made it." Jay describes himself as unassuming, quiet, thoughtful and good looking. Here's looking at you, Jay! Club: The Mud Club at The Subway. Record: 'Status Quo' by Donald Banks.

**RUSTY EGAN** – Club Entrepreneur & Record Producer. First appeared in i-D NO.2. The Rich Kids, The Blitz, Club For Heroes, The Camden Palace, The Playground etc... "The 80s have meant the setting up of my three companies... and basically I'm still crazy after all these years. 1985 has been just like 1975 and I can't wait for 77. I'm 27, single, do what I want to do... and it's brilliant! In five years time I want to find another Blitz." Club: The Roof Gardens ("There's always a party there!"). Record: "Anything by U2, they're brilliant."

**JANE KHAN** – Fashion Designer. First appeared in i-D NO.6. Now Khaniverous, then Khan & Bell... Jane is Birmingham's answer to Barbarella. "Armageddon missed us this year, but who knows? Myself I've become younger but wiser... and this year has been very successful – playing hard and working hard. In five years time I hope to be able to spend more time on designing and I'd like to open shops in Tokyo, Sydney and New York." Jane is arty. Club: "The Hippodrome and The Sanctuary for the morning after." Record: Cristina – 'Is That All There Is?'.

**MICHAEL CLARK** – Dancer. First appeared in i-D NO.28. The darling of modern dance, he has the best looking pair of legs in the business. "I am changeable, but in five years I'd like to be doing exactly the same as I am now. Nothing has really been outstanding about the last five years, but 1985 will look good in 1986." Club: Princess Julia & The Love Groins. Record: "Anything by Joni Mitchell."

**JOHN CRANCHER** – Fashion Designer. First appeared ... Connoisseur of the male romantic look – satin and orga[nza] ... last five years have been important because I've started ... and find out where I'm going. My hair's changed quite a ... changed much – I'm just as boring as ever." John thin[ks] ... "colourful", and would like to be an i-D journalist in f[ive] ... Club: Planets. Record: 'Sugar Sugar' – Tasty Tim.

**STEVE STRANGE** – Nightclub Entrepreneur, Singer. First appeared in i-D No. 2. The instigator of the 80s as we know them... who, along with Rusty Egan started a night at Billy's Nightclub and never looked back. The 80s?: "It started off great with Visage and 'Fade To Grey' but by the third album I was ready to pack everything in and go and live in Japan. It was OK running nightclubs and having a good time, but a lot of people in the nightclub scene are so false and you have a lot of hangers on..." Club: "I suppose you will think I'm being egotistical, but if Rusty Egan and I hadn't started The Blitz, a lot of nightclubs happening now would never have taken off." Record: "'The Russians' from the Sting album."

**CARYN FRANKLIN & NICK TRULOCKE** Fashion Editor & Club Entrepeneur. Frankie, she of the radiant smile and short temper & Nick: bar-prop, womaniser & BMW driver. Nick: "The most important thing that's happened to me in the last five years was getting my girlfriend Caryn into bed for the first time. It took six months and cost me a fortune in candlelit dinners." Caryn: "In five years I want to have mastered the art of getting cross properly. 1985 was the year that Swatch took over the world, David Holah kissed Neil Kinnock... and i-D opened more eyes than ever." Club: Taboo/DoDos. Record: George McCrae – 'Its Been So Long.'

**DAVID JOHNSON** – Journalist with The London Standard. First appeared in i-D No. 2. David was one of the first commentators on the Blitz scene. "The Blitz Kids still deserve more recognition for having sparked off one of postwar Britain's most potent subcultures. It has not only united several generations of the new casually working class, but also led them to more choice, better taste and a voice – that voice starting with i-D and Channel 4. The blaggers and liggers really must start thinking bigger than their next club, record and haircut – making serious noises in the corridors of power. 1985?: The year the style supermarket repackaged the previous four as an over-the-counter-culture." Club: The Blue Note, Derby in 1982. Record: Rhoda Dakar's 'The Boiler', Spandau Ballet's 'Chant No. 1'.

**CHRISTOS TOLERA** – Singer & Interior Decorator. First appeared in i-D No. 1. One of the warblers in Blue Rondo, Christos certainly knows how to drink! And then some! "I'm a great bloke... who's been known to be a perfectionist. We're now on the verge, everything's on the verge. There's been a saturation of fashion, and it's difficult to distinguish the good people from the wallies. Before the 80s, all we had to read was women's magazines, but now we've got things like i-D and Channel 4. Real sex is gonna come back in a big way, as are girls wearing less make-up and men wearing none at all. Me? I've become a lot busier but more pessimistic." Club: St Moritz. Record: "Anything by Blue Rondo."

**HELEN ROBINSON** – Fashion Designer and owner of PX. First appeared in i-D No. 9. Par Excellence has been one of the most influential shops in the world, from the camouflage and cowboys of early days in James Street... all the way up to today. "Having a baby is the most fundamental thing to happen to me," she says. "In five years, I'd like to be doing what I'm doing now but making some money out of it." Helen depicts herself as "serious". "All I've got in the last five years is older." Club: Bain Douche in Paris. Record: 'Spacer' – Sheila B. Devotion.

**JALLE BAKKE** – Make Up Artist. First appeared in i-D No. ... talented and incredibly talented. The 80s: "People have b[een] ... their individuality... times make it easy for people to ... interesting things. We have taken the best things from ... and remodelled them for the 80s. I am much more p[o]... about things. I don't care what the neighbours think any ... been a year where I've done my most exciting work. I've ... respect for who I am and what I do." Jalle describe[s] ... "Psychedelic sunflower." Club: The Pink Panther. Rec[ord] ... Mega-Mix.

FIVE YEAR CELEBRATION

i-D

19

Francesca wears: Black Joseph Tricot leggings £18; Martin Kidman rust jumper £395; Joseph Tricot black top with hood, £69; Doc Martens £25 from Joseph; hat courtesy of Joseph.

CHECK OUT SLOANE ST
The Joseph shops, the relaunched Harrods Way In, and the crunchy nouveaux nouvelle cuisinerie of the Joseph cafe at the Pour La Maison shop.

Tracy wears: Blue skirt £65; Polo jumper £89; Cardi £110; Grey coat £139; Cream leggings £18 – all Joseph Tricot. Katharine Hamnett white silk shirt £69. Shoes from a selection at Hackett, from £17.

Lisa wears Riffat Ozbeck trousers £92, coat with furry hood £439, poloneck top £139, "Parfum Du Jour" T-shirt approx. £20, all from Joseph. Shoes from a selection at Hackett, from £17.

STYLING BY **CAROLINE BAKER**, PHOTOGRAPHED BY **EAMONN J McCABE**. MODELS JOSEPH STAFF.

AND WILLIAM
JENNY, CHRIS, NICK AND JAMES
ARTHUR CURTIS
MARGARITA
JOSH AND HEINI
ANNE
MABEL STRÖM
EDWARD
HILL HOUSE SCHOOL
JIM
MICHAEL
MATSA

– Pop Singer. First appeared in i-D NO.5. Former Reluctant – now King big-wig. "Today I am the same person but more, and in five years time I would like to become a 'Man of the improve my ability. 1985 has been a year of Love and Pride." 80s?: "Meeting Perry and the boys in King." Club: Dial 9 For cord: "I like so many."

**SCARLETT** – Model. First appeared in i-D No. 2. Scarlett was the face that every foreign magazine photographed when they catalogued the Blitz scene. From Sydney to Scandinavia… "My dog, Cerebus, is the best thing that's happened to me. I've grown up a bit and I'm not an alcoholic anymore – I'm very nice these days… even if I am a bit bossy." 1985: "Quite fabulous." In 60 months' time, Scarlett wants to be extremely rich, extremely successful and a TV superstar. Club: Cha Cha. Record: "I don't know anything about music."

**TOM BINNS** – Jewellery Designer. First appeared in i-D No.18. The Irish cool cat intent on subverting the world with his creations. "In the 80s I've started to make money, I've become richer and in five years I hope I'm retired. I am a quiet and lovable person. 1985 has been a year of constipation and toilet rolls." Club: Noel & Maurice at Battlebridge Road. Record: 'Drop The Bomb' – Trouble Funk.

**ALICE RYCROFT** – Fashion Designer. First appeared in i-D No. 20. Since leaving St Martin's, Alice has cut her hair and cornered the market with her Captain Scarlett clothes for boys and girls. "I've not changed much really, because I'm not much of an extrovert. I'd really like to go into space on my own – to boldly go where no man has gone before." She

**MARTIN FRY** – Singer/Songwriter. First appeared in i-D No. 8. As the frontman to ABC, Martin has travelled the world with his hand on his heart. "The 80s have seen the magnificent birth of New York musical culture – Electro, Hip-Hop, Scratching and Breakdancing – a true revelation. I've got richer and grown two inches… though I'm not saying where. In five years' time I'd like to be cutting a disc and crooning on a cruiser to the moon – sheer poetry!" Martin says he is "Faithful and full of faith." Club: Wigwam/Hacienda. Record: 'Padlock' – Gwen Guthrie.

**SOPHIE HICKS** – Fashion Journalist. First appeared in i-D NO.16. Grace Coddington's assistant, then Tatler bod, now back at Vogue. Best thing about the 80s?: "Meeting Marc Boxer." How have you changed?: "I've given up skirts." 5 years time?: "Travelling the world." 1985?: "Hard work." Sophie is pushy. Club: Soul Furnace. Record: 'Hit Me With Your Rhythm Stick' – Ian Dury & The Blockheads.

ANO – Fashion Designer. First appeared in i-D No. 21. Left St ummer 84, mammoth Olympia show in spring 85, worldwide 86. Most important event of the decade?: "Pearly King & ding down the Charing Cross Road." 1985: "A marvellous, ear." In five years' time, John expects to be rich, famous and lse that goes with it. He describes himself as "Yes, no, yes, be." Club: Taboo. Record: 'Everything She Wants' – Wham!

**ANDY CZEZOWSKI & JIMMY FOX** – Club Entrepreneur & Club Performer, respectively. First appeared in i-D's NO.19 & 13. Fridge owners both!! Andy: "The seeds of the next decade have been sown, as they were in 65 & 75. We are strengthening our resolve to combat the system and in years to come I want to be in charge of the Brixton principality." Jimmy: "I've got into showbiz and become show-bizzy – I am very talented." Andy: "We are the diamonds in the sewers of life." Club: The Fridge/Scandals. Record: The Smiths – 'Barbarism'/Marilyn – 'You Don't Love Me.'

**LIZZY TIER** – Singer. First appeared in i-D No. 4. Former model, now singer of tantalising talents. "The most important happening of recent times was 'The Great Rock And Roll Swindle'. Myself, I've left school, grown taller, my hair has grown longer and my lungs have got bigger. In five years' time I hope I'm recording an LP in a studio in Bali." Lizzy is serious at work, a permanent playster, and very cunning indeed… "What we need is a revolution!" Club: Do-Dos ("All the good clubs are dead."). Record: 'Moments In Love' – Art Of Noise.

**WILLIAM FALKNER** – Make Up Artist. First appeared in i-D NO.25. Slap addict supreme, William is American. "The 80s for me meant moving to London and telling my boyfriend I love him … and losing one wisdom tooth. In five years time I hope I'm counting all my money." William is …"Incredibly handsome." Club: The Trap in San Francisco. Record: 'Everything She Wants' – Wham!

**SIMON FORBES** – Hairdresser and creator of Antenna. First appeared in i-D No. 7. One of the most influential cutters of our times, his hair-pieces have caused sensations all over the place. Ace! "I think that 1985 is the year that it happened for a lot of people – in the past five years I've grown up and become more flexible, more aware of the realities of life. In five years' time I'd like to be living anywhere else apart from London – I've lived here for 15 years and I'm sick of it. I would describe myself as a pain in the arse." Club: Dial 9 For Dolphin. Record: 'Hunters & Collectors'.

**JUDY BLAME** – Jewellery Designer. First appeared in i-D No. 6. Chris' creations have been acknowledged worldwide – a veritable star. "My career is the most important thing that's happened… ever. And I've just got madder. 1985 has been a peak for me personally… I'm very content – I hope I'm doing the same thing in five years' time." Club: Taboo. Record: 'Do You Really Want To Hurt Me?' – Culture Club.

TONY

· Stylist. First appeared in i-D No. 16. The supreme Buffalo pork-pie hats, big lapel jackets and 'Killer' cards have streets of London from Soho to Ladbroke Grove. "The 80s consolidating friendships. Today I have less hair… but I'm 985?: "The year of i-D." 1990?: "In that year I hope I'll be fourth feature film." Club: Paradise Garage in New York. God, Mi King' – Phillip Levi.

**JOHN RICHMOND & MARIA CORNEJO** – Fashion Designers. First appeared in i-D Nos. 18 and 13 respectively. Jesus & Mary are the designer darlings of 1985, what with their affiliation with Joseph and their extraordinary skirts and zips. The best happening in the 1980s?: John – "Richmond/Cornejo." Maria – "Meeting J.R. (not Ewing)." How hast thou changed?: John – "Seen too much and learnt too little." Maria – "I've become more cynical and cellulite." Five years' time?: John – "Putting money into different things." Maria – "Retired with a good pension." Yourself?: John – "A dreamer (out to win)." Maria – "Beautiful." Club: Taboo/The Mickey Mouse Club. Record: 'Bladerunner' – Vangelis.

**TONY WILSON** – TV Presenter, Record Mogul and Club Owner. First appeared in i-D No. 4. Tony is a regular Granada talking head, the brains and money behind Factory Records and Manchester's Hacienda. He carries a shoulder-bag. "The 80s began with me subsiding from my level of cultural excitement – but then the influence of China, Hip Hop and fatherhood made me more excited, excitable and committed than before. In 1990 I'd like to be not selling a single vinyl record and to be a star on TV in New York." Tony calls himself a "bastard". Club: Hacienda. Record: "Nothing in the 80s has yet superseded Joy Division's 'Atmosphere'."

**RACHEL AUBURN** – Fashion Designer. First appeared in i-D No. 23. Spend, Spend, Spend is the title of Rachel's company… she is an inveterate doyenne of style (she also DJs at Taboo). 1980s?: "It's seen the development of my work. I've got more confident and a lot better at what I do. I'm adventurous, I'm strong and I'm hard. OK!? I can't possibly think about what I'll be doing in five years' time. 1985? Static." Club: Taboo. Record: 'Vishnu' – West India Company.

**NEIL SPENCER** – Journalist. First appeared in i-D No. 22. Neil was editor of the NME between Nick Logan and Ian Pye, initiating the infamous NME cassettes, and broader editorial issues. He's a politically aware lad. "I'm a happier man 'cos I've calmed down, lightened up, made some very good new friends and I haven't forgotten how to dance." Describing himself as an ageing Mod, Neil says "Things have got a lot worse for most people, but the mood and atmosphere is a lot more optimistic – people have discovered a source of hope that they didn't have a couple of years ago. The most important thing that's happened recently is the proliferation of nuclear arms." Club: Hot Sty. Record: 'Ami' – Bebe Manga. 'Thriller' – Michael Jackson.

**SIMON FOXTON** – Stylist & Fashion Designer. First appeared in i-D No. 13. The original brains behind Bazooka, Simon now styles for a living. "The most important thing about the 80s for me was love and romance – lots of it. I now have less hair and a muscle… and I enjoy beachcombing. 1985 has been the year of figs and more figs." Club: The Lift at Stallions. Record: 'Apollo' by Brian Eno… or anything by Michael Nyman.

i-D No. 37 1986 ph. Nick Knight stylist Simon Foxton

## 46

**S**

Urban paranoia surrounds the rumour that London club-runners are re-introducing William The Conqueror's 'Scorch Policy' of burning down hostels of rebellion, or in this case, *competition*. Wearing their hearts on their sleeves and their heroes on the backs of their MA1 Army jackets these nightclub entrepreneurs roam the streets appalled at this wanton disco arson. Will they be next to suffer the wrath of the West One Scorchers? The Soviet butterflies cast their competitors' flyers into the remnants of yet another venue. . . and wonder.

Photograph Nick Knight
Styling Simon Foxton

Black jackets £20 approx, from all Camping and Army shops. Woven Chinese patches £3 each from Gung Ho Book Shop, Gerrard St, London W1. 501's Levis natural (kindly donated by Levis for the ripping off) approx £30, available from Jean Jeanie Oxford St and selected branches through the country, Western Frontier in Selfridges London W1 and Way In at Harrods.

From left to right - EDDIE, TONY, LISTON, VERNON and JAMES.

hundred watt bulb for the front, one for the back, two months, and you can do it over there in the corner. I'd been lighting portraits with torches and putting flames in the background and using half hour exposures, and from that story I learn how to appreciate lighting with one simple source.

Terry pushed me to get past the foibles and tricks which photographers like to fall back on. Photographers look at the craft rather than the content of a picture, but he insists that human energy is the most important thing a picture can have, not the colour range, or the quality of the lighting. The first story I shot for 'Vogue', with art director Robin Derrick (another 'i-D' graduate), was for the Glamour is Back issue. In one of the last stories Terry did at 'Vogue' he had the models aiming a flash-gun direct into camera, and we did the same. It was a nod and a wink to Terry."

I frequently work with graphic designers who have an illustrative ability that I have never had the patience for. Steve Male came to my studio as an illustrator with virtually no knowledge of type, and became my right-hand-man at "i-D". Moira Bogue, who came to my studio to write her college thesis, stayed for five years. The end results are infinite, as various assistants who are responsible for the final layouts add their personal style to each job.

Moira Bogue, ex "i-D" art editor: "Every day Terry would come in with different ideas or feelings about a job or story. This was the most challenging aspect of working with him, but it's also his special quality. Every day he'd bring in something or someone fresh, to keep ideas moving, no matter where they came from or how they got there - quite serendipitous, light and buoyant."

Neil Edwards, ex-"i-D" art editor: "After leaving the Royal College of Art I learnt more in an afternoon with Terry than in five years of art school. He is always challenging and questioning, as he comes from the make-it-up-as-you-go-along school. He could be a pain in the arse sometimes but it was certainly an experience. He would get photographers to design layouts, journalists to take pictures, designers to write articles. He'd get us all swapping roles to see what happened, but then he has a talent for harmonising the anarchy and creating a continual evolution rather than set museum pieces. Terry's like a little design storm-trooper, parachuting in and getting things rolling. You could drop him in the middle of a jungle with just a pencil stub and within a few days he'd have the head-hunters producing a newsletter out of bark and animal droppings - probably! I think everyone that's worked with him is like a disciple spreading his anarchic gospel - all of us unemployable but having a laugh none the less."

...the vanities!

THE SUBVERSIVE ISSUE    NO.141

cover star: shalom harlow photographed by craig mcdean  june1995

# i-D

©

i-DEAS, FASHION, CLUBS, MUSIC, PE

52 **supergrass, menswear & indie's boy babes**

**the panthers reawaken black america**

**why aliens are taking over the world**

**clubland's next generation**

# No More Heroes
## ARE SUPERMODELS OUT OF FASHION?

£2.20  $5.50

06

9 770262 357020

FRANCS 38 LIRE 9,000 DM 13,50 PESETAS 625 D KR 59

cover star kiara photographed by craig mcdean january 1995

©

**i-DEAS, FASHION, CLUBS, MUSIC, PEOPLE**

# THIS IS THE
# FUTURE!
## life in cyberspace

**the black dog • policing the internet**

**future shock fashion • cyborgfeminism**

**a guy called gerald • techno subversives**

**£2.20   $5.50**

9 770262 357020

FRANCS 38 LIRE 10,000 DM 13,50 PESETAS 625 D KR 59

**Ben** wears satin Chinese shirt by Joe Casely-Hayford from Jones, 13 Floral St, London WC2, Hip, 14 Thornton's Arcade, Leeds and Substance, 7 High Bridge St, Newcastle-Upon-Tyne, and customised Levi's jeans.

**Ben** wears vest from Souled Out, Unit 25, Portobello Arcade, London W10, satin pants by Joe Casely-Hayford from Jones, 13 Floral St, London WC2, Hip, 14 Thornton's Arcade, Leeds and Substance, 7 High Bridge St, Newcastle-Upon-Tyne.

**Ben** wears woven vest and cotton pants by Yohji Yamamoto from Richard Creme, 1/2 Barton Arcade, Manchester.

# strictly

## SUMMER FASHION

PHOTOGRAPHY BY **TRAVIS**
STORY BY **SIMON FOXTON**
STYLING ASSISTANCE AND CASTING BY **EDWARD ENNINFUL**
THANKS TO **CRAIG McDEAN** AND **ANDREW NEWMAN**

*"No perfumes... but very fine linen, plenty of it and country washing. If John Bull turns round to look after you, you are not well dressed; but either too stiff, too tight or too fashionable."* Beau Brummell

**Sam** wears jacket from Portobello Market, shirt from Polo, Ralph Lauren, scarf by Hysteric Glamour available to order on 071 224 2656, cotton riding trousers from Swaine & Adeney and suede shoes by House Of Beauty & Culture available from The Dispensary.

David wears shirt by Matsuda available from Yuzo, trousers from Yohji Yamamoto (available from September), shoes by House Of Beauty & Culture available from The Dispensary and velvet choker ribbon from John Lewis.
Detail of pink shirt by G-Fay from Dispensary.

Edward wears jacket and plus twos from Swaine & Adeney, poloneck from The Dispensary, shoes from Trickers, monocle on chain from Chanel and bracelet model's own.

Throughout its history "i-D" has nurtured the talents of people who were starting out, and has sometimes totally altered the course of the career they thought they were heading for...amongst others, Caryn Franklin, a graphic designer turned fashion guru; Simon Foxton, fashion designer to style-king; Dylan Jones, graphic designer to prolific writer and editor! Talent breeds talent, as assistants to one generation of "i-D" contributors become the next. Judy Blame and Simon Foxton were mentors for a whole influx of stylists. Edward Enninful was one of Foxton's proteges when Simon recommended him to my then fashion editor, Beth Summers, who had in turn assisted Caryn Franklin. By the age of nineteen Edward was fashion editor of the magazine. Marc Lebon, photographer: "I introduced Judy Blame and Ray Petri, both influencial stylists, to 'i-D'. I think of myself as someone who re-presents. The clothes, models and stylists, they're the cake, the content, and the artistry of photography is only the icing, bottom of the list. Terry taught me not to be too precious, to be open to other people's needs so that you remain a student, green, and in the end you become a wiser person."
For the period when I was working at Esprit I asked Nick Knight if he would become picture editor at "i-D". Nick's reputation and association with "i-D" made him the best choice for the job and I was really pleased that he accepted. I wanted to make sure the standard of photographic innovation remained high and Nick elevated the quality of the photographic contributions whilst also organising the

compilation of "i-D"'s tenth anniversary issue portfolio. Many photographers who began their careers at "i-D" have become major influences in fashion photography: Ellen Von Unwerth, David Sims, Juergen Teller, Wolfgang Tillmans, Craig McDean.
Magazine art direction is about getting it right before anyone goes out on a photo-shoot. It's about putting people together. Using someone new is taking a chance but that chance is calculated on my understanding and experience. At the point that I decide someone is right for the job, for their first break, I believe absolutely that they are capable of doing it. I need to meet the photographer face to face, to get the best results because I'm interested in how they think and their passions. How they react to me is a good indication of how they will respond to the people they photograph.
I've reacted against the photographers' myth that you have to be a bastard to get a good picture. The 60s and 70s school of fashion photography was about intimidation, and manipulating people.
When I started on "Vanity Fair", I was very influenced by the photographer Frank Horvat. One of the lessons Horvat taught me was that the position of the photographer is open for abuse but if you want a humanitarian result you have to encourage people to participate and "give" you the picture. Horvat made me understand the power of approval. I want the subject to be respected, always.

D.C. Lee

Having just completed her latest album, under the guise of Slam Slam with collaborators Dr Robert, mentor and Paul Weller, her latest single 'Something Ain't Right' was released on October 1st, the Album 'Free The Feeling' will be released shortly.
Hipster canvas jeans by Lee, short sleeve white with blue and red stripes on sleeve top from Estase From Havana, Kensington Market and Adidas Shell tops from Passenger.
Original Wrangler rope button blue cord jacket and beige hipsters.

Paul Weller

Currently recording in his Solid Bond Studios, he has just completed the band line-up for his international tour commencing in November. With a single planned for release in February 1991, the musical direction remains a closely guarded secret but names like Broken R + B and Space Mode are more than just code names.
Original i-Spy style bright orange short sleeve top, white Levi 502 skirts from Japan and Adidas suede tops from hip land.
Original Marks & Spencer crew neck, paisley jacket courtesy of Mick Talbot, slacks unknown source and black suede loafers.

Richard Okon
*Photographer*
Original US Levi 501s,
John Smedley from
Woodhouse, Loafers
from J. Simons and US
check jacket from
American Classics
Richard 'Young Rich'
Okon is recently back
from New York, with
uncensored tapes of
Muslim discourse, the
contents of which
have not yet been
made public.

professional tennis player and sidekick, the global adventures of US Government agents Culp and Cosby (the antithesis to the 'Men From UNCLE' in more ways than one) are littered with mishaps and misrepresentations, a world where the bad guys are not always bad and where the best man doesn't always win. Sure, Scott was nowhere to be seen on the opening credits, and agreed, he never got the girl, despite being multilingual beyond belief; but in a time of apartheid in the Southern states, of racial inequality throughout the US.

Market, a car boot sale in Penge, a sports shop in Cardiff - uncovering the sources relied on luck, a lot of leg work and word of mouth. Gradually, however, certain reliable outlets are beginning to appear: notably the Crazy Clothes Connection in Rye Lane, south London and Escape From Havana, Kensington Market. Other sources remain pretty much close to their chests... this message will not self destruct...

**Andrew Levy** - musician: Brand New Heavies/K-Collective.
'Anthony Turner' shirt/jacket from the 'Killer' collection and original hand made ste-press trousers.
Andy, with his partner (Jan Kincaid) have been rumoured to be the Steely and Cleave of the British funk scene. Andrew is the thumping bass player for the Brand New Heavies.

Group shots taken during the regular monthly Hardtimes club night at The Pyramid Arts Centre, 10/16 Ashwin St, Dalston. The next Hardtimes event is Saturday 27th October.

# i-D

THE BORN AGAIN ISSUE

## i-D MAGAZINE
i-DEAS, FASHION, CLUBS, MUSIC, PEOPLE

**tear it up!**

MICA PARIS — BORN AGAIN SOUL

**Robert De Niro and Martin Scorsese interviewed** ● **The new breed of trainers** ● **Cult watching - protecting the spiritual consumer** ● **Bruce Sterling and William Gibson - from cyberpunk to steampunk** ● **Permaculture - gardening as guerilla warfare** ● **Phil 'Reflecting Skin' Ridley - sick as a frog?** ● **i-Spy Fashion - Radical Modernists**

9 770262 357006    11

USA $5.50

FRANCS 33 LIRE 5,900 DM12.50 PESETAS 665 D KR 49

THE HARD ISSUE

# i-D

i-DEAS, FASHION, CLUBS, MUSIC, PEOPLE

122 november 1993

i-D

cover star: linda evangelista

# XTRA HARD!

BAD GIRLS: SHAVED, PIERCED, TATTOOED

## RIGHT SAID FRED
### PJ HARVEY/FRESH PRINCE
## FUTURE SOUND OF LONDON
### SCOOTERS RIDE AGAIN!/THE NEW RAP POETS

£1.95    $4.95

9 770262 357013    11

FRANCS 35 LIRE 7,100 DM 13,00 PESETAS 595 D KR 53

**FASHION SPECIAL**
# INTRODUCING NEW YORK'S NEW COOL

i-DEAS, FASHION, CLUBS, MUSIC, PEOPLE

**OCEAN COLOUR SCENE
IS DRUG TESTING
TAKING THE PISS?
HEAD RUSH: SPORT'S
NEW HARD LINE
THIS THUG'S LIFE: THE
LEGACY OF TUPAC
EVAN DANDO ON OASIS
BOMBING THE BASS
IN BOSNIA**

# pure sexy!

£2.20    $5.75

**JUERGEN TELLER SHOOTS TO SCORE**

9 770262 357020

FRANCS 38 LIRE 9,000 DM 13,50 PESETAS 625 D KR 59

Grey herring-bone tweed double-breasted overcoat from John Pearse and black felt trilby from Herbert Johnson.

Dark grey tweed coat from Portobello Market.

# paradise lost?
# Românîa

## SPRING 1990

You don't have to be guilty to suffer punishment.

Story by Juergen Teller and Venetia Scott
Thanks to Mikail Bedrada, The Volosinovicis, Eugenia and Kira Jolliffe

FORMATIE SI REPORTAJ

i-D THE PARADISE ISSUE 47

*natural* fashion

PHOTOGRAPHY BY JUERGEN TELLER
STYLING BY VENETIA SCOTT
ASSISTED BY ROSE RAINEY
HAIR AND MAKE-UP BY DAVID GRAINGER
THANKS TO TEAM MANAGEMENT, SYDNEY
SHOT AT TONTABLE FALLS, NIMBIN, AUSTRALIA

In the community of New South Wales, a subtropical climate, regular rainfall and abundant food means you take life one day at a time. Very slowly.

It's not called Paradise Valley for nothing...

*nadine*

Kersten wears antique cotton petticoat from Crazy Clothing Connection, 134-136 Lancaster Road, London W11.

## love and hate

# COURTNEY LOVE IS MORE FAMOUS FOR HER HUSBAND AND HER MOUTHINESS THAN HER BAND, HOLE. HER NEW ALBUM MIGHT CHANGE ALL THAT - BUT WILL IT MAKE COURTNEY HAPPY?

Courtney Love-Cobain looks elegantly fucked up. Casting aside her plain black everyday attire, she straps on a pair of high-heeled sandals, shakes loose her bleached-out hair, and wraps her dangerously curvy frame in a battered satin dress. Her green eyes are heavily made up. Her mouth, an overstated gash of scarlet, seems both vulgar and sensual. Courtney's fingernails, chipping crimson, are chewed down to ragged skin. She's tired, so tired. When she pauses, her eyes narrow to a sleepy sexiness. Taking a deep sigh, she places a glittering foot onto the white curve of the photographer's backdrop and transforms herself for the camera, from artist, wife and mother into Courtney Love, bruised temptress. She looks like an embodiment of anti-feminist mythology reincarnated as the bad girl of rock. She has become Courtney Love, Celebrity.

What happened to Courtney Love reads less like a career structure, more a chapter from *Hollywood Babylon*. The worst thing is that everyone wants to believe it, all of it. They've come to expect nothing less. There's no middle ground: as has been said before, Courtney Love is not so much a character to be interviewed as a cause to be championed - or a witch to be burned. Confusion is what she thrives on. People either love her or hate her, their reactions as extreme as her challenges. Drama follows Courtney Love close behind.

You know that already of course, or at least you do if you have any degree of media-literacy at all. You know she was introduced to Britain by Nirvana's Kurt Cobain, who announced to millions via *The Word* that she was "the best fuck in the world". You know she married him and had a baby

PHOTOGRAPHY BY ELLEN VON UNWERTH STYLING BY ANDREW RICHARDSON ASSISTED BY DEVRA KINNERY HAIR BY WARD AT BRYAN BANTRY MAKE-UP BY SUSAN STERLING AT FORD HAIR AND BEAUTY

62

Eva Herzigova i-D No. 155 August 1996 ph. Ellen von Unwerth

cover star: **björk** photographed by ellen von unwerth **SEPTEMBER 1994**

# i-D

© 

**i-DEAS, FASHION, CLUBS, MUSIC, PEOPLE**

## INTERNATIONAL STREET FASHION SPECIAL

paranoia in cyberspace

the future for football

Massive Attack

Shed Seven

Rebel MC

the best disco dancing guide in the world

**public enemy**
### Chuck D in the dock

russell simmons
### Hip hop's top dog

the drum club
### Trance tripping in Tokyo

# björk!
## A Night Out With Miss World

£2.20  $5.50

09

9 770262 357020

FRANCS 38 LIRE 10,000 DM 13,50 PESETAS 625 D KR 59

i-D

i-DEAS, FASHION, CLUBS, MUSIC, PEOPLE

9 770262 357020

04

Sex!

Success!

All-American

Excess!

COURTNEY

comes clean

ECSTASY

Is there

still

something

you don't

know?

**NAJIM** is an actor and a musician and gets straight down to the latest dance craze the Kerb Crawl. His fave toon is 'Get to this get to that ' by Sly and Robbie and he likes to shake a leg to this at Balajo, rue de Lappe. He ain't got time for people who don't do anything with their time.

**Jeans and raincoat by Liberto. Socks from Surplus Bensimon and Pumps from Stemm.**

**ISIS** is a singer and unaware of any resemblance she bears to Brigitte Bardot even though she does. She likes Tina Turner and Mick Jagger and she loves to dance, to laugh and to Love and she hates Tax.

**Dress by York and Cole.**

PHOTOGRAPHY BY ELLEN VON UNSWERTH. STYLING BY CORINNE NOELLA. MAKE-UP BY TRACY MARTIN. HAIR BY LUCIO.

PHOTOGRAPHY BY
TERRY RICHARDSON
CLAUDIA AND
ELEANOR WEAR
GUESS JEANS
CHRISTIAN WEARS
SECONDHAND LEVI'S
SHIRT **Christian
Wooley**, 24,
actor. **Fragrance?**
Yves Saint Laurent
**Last thing you take
off at night?** Boots
**First thing you put on
in the morning?**
Boots **Where are
you happiest naked?**
The supermarket
**Who would you
most like to
undress?** Madonna

erry Richardson, photographer. Wears secondhand clothes, K-Mart shoes nd Woolworth's watch. **What makes life worth living?** Nikki **If you had one ish...** To have a 15 inch penis **Why are you in NYC?** It's so damn Shiek **Nikki berti**, 'My age? Don't even go there with me', model. Wears secondhand othes. **What makes life worth living?** Terry **If you had one wish...** I'll have hat he's having! **Why are you in NYC?** That's where the action is, baby!

**Iris Palmer**, 19, model. Wears dress and shoes from Portobello Market, Sock Shop tights and Phillip Treacy hat. **Favourite Record?** *I Feel A Car Crash Coming On* by Sharkbait **Favourite place in London?** My flat **Best thing about living in London?** My friends

# WATER SPORTS

Tribes, n'teams, cults n'crews for all the gang. With intensive training and a life
jacket you too could share the thrills and spills of group activities, like the bold
bunch featured: formation ski-ing is the 'Wow' sport in Tomahawk, Wisconsin-State,
U.S.A. Yes it's Martini, waterproof make up-and tom tom club rapping the beat at the
Kwahamot club (that's Tomahawk backwards of course). Photographed by Tim Holt

# MEANWHILE ON THE OTHER SIDE OF THE ATLANTIC

### NEW YORK

SQUARE CITY AND DULL LIFE. THE BUBBLES ARE ALL GONE. NO MORE HANGING OUT THE WAY
IT USED TO BE. NOW THAT NEW WAVE BECAME COMMERCIAL, THOSE WHO HAVE MADE IT OVER
THE PAST THREE YEARS ARE NOW TOO BUSY WORKING? FINALLY EXPLOITING THE TREND LIKE
ANY GOOD BUSINESSLIKE BODY ELSE.

BUT WHERE ARE THE BUBBLES GONE? ROCK AND ROLL IS DYING, NOTHING NEW AND CABARET/
COMEDY IS MAKING A STRONG AND NOTICEABLE COME BACK: THE MUSIC USUALLY SUCKS AND
PROPS. BACK SINGERS AND ACTS MAKE THE PILL EASIER TO SWALLOW, AND THE SHOWS MORE
BEARABLE TO WATCH. RATHER UNPROFESSIONAL AND ENTERTAINING. NOT AT ALL PRETENTIOUS
AND HILARIOUS CUZ IT'S SO BAD... BUT... THERE IS SOMETHING ALMOST NEW COMING FROM
THE SOUTH BRONX. THE MOST GHETTO BOROUGH OF NEW YORK CITY. THEY RAP UP THERE AND
THEY START COMING DOWNTOWN. THEY LOOK TOUGH AND THEY ARE THE LAST ONES TO HAVE
SOME TYPE OF ENERGY.

THE VISUAL ARTS ARE MORE INTERESTING: PAINTINGS ARE BRIGHT AND FRESH AND NAIVE AND
THREE DIMENSIONAL, AND THE "IS THAT GARBAGE ART?" HAS BEEN MOVING OUT OF ITS GUTTER
ALTERNATIVE SPACES TO MORE ESTABLISHED 57TH STREET AND SOHO GALLERIES. EVERYBODY
IS AN ARTIST IN THIS CITY BUT THE HARD CORE BELONGS TO COLLABORATIVE PROJECTS, INC.
S.V.P. A GROUP OF THE LOWER LOWER EAST SIDE WHO INC. ED TO GET SUBSIDES FROM WASH-
INGTON AGENCIES. THEY ARE NO LONGER UNDERGROUND BUT TRY TO LOCATE THEIR MANIFESTO,
ANIMAL LIVING IN THE CITY AND OTHER SHOWS, GOOD LUCK...

WHERE ARE YOU FROM? BELGIUM, RUSSIA AND ALBANIA, THEY ARE ALL FROM OUTER SPACE AND
SOME FOREIGN COUNTRIES.

THEY ARE THE NEW ELITE, THE NEW WAVE OF IMMIGRANTS OVERFLOWING THE CITY BUT UNLIKE
THE OTHER SCUM OF THE EARTH WHO CAME EARLIER, THEY ARE WHITE, EDUCATED AND CHARMING.
THEY ARE INTERJECTING SOME NEW BLOOD BADLY NEEDED INTO A COUNTRY RAISED ON HORMON
CHICKEN AND VITAMINE-D MILK. LIVING OFF THE LAND, NO ONE BOTHERS WITH THEM AS LONG
AS THEY HAVEN'T MADE IT THE MAIN REASON TO COME TO THIS COUNTRY AND FOR THE I.R.S.
TO LOOK AFTER ANYONE. Sophie V.D.T.

TOMY GUN and fashion the very last of the punks, he droped his safety pin six
months ago for a greasy beehive. Back to the old values, leather and square-
ness.

SUSAN ANGST, modelling for $10 000 jobs or selling at Bloomingdale's for $69.75
a week. Too much corruption to deal with and no one to count on but herself.
Need a wooden head to hold it together, or a farm like the one she will get soon

# ROCK 'N' ROLLERS

ROCK N'ROLLERS-A SOUTH SI-DE STORY
Rock n'Rollers skate on weekends in Battersea Park.Adrenalin and
skill the buzz of being'tops'is realized through team sports and
a competitive craze!Colours n'slogans,symbols n'style designate
who you're rolling with.

# Bikini Ballet

# BRIGHTON SPARKS

The thing is that we want to do a ballet on Brighton
beach,with a large lot of people in it.At first we
were going to ask everybody in the college to be in
it but that might have been a bit ambitious,so we
pared our plans down a bit,and decided on just getting
as many people as we could.We approached BETTE and she
said that there was a trip to Brighton organized for
June.perfect.You may feel a little unnerved about the
idea of being in a ballet because it's usually done by
tall lean things in frilly lace & jock straps,but that
is the whole rub about ballet why should it be done
by good arian types,why not old people,children,plump
people with spots or even people without any sense of
rythmn?Ballet may be about the glorification of the
body and movement but what's wrong with mine or yours
they've got more in common with the audiences than
any classical performers.Anyway I want to be in a
ballet just for the fun of it,and this seems like a
good oportunity.So this ballet isn't reallly a ballet
in the Rambert sense it's more alot of people taking
part in an event,like Rugby League or group sex.MASS
BALLET WITHOUT RYTHMN & WITH IMPROVISATION so you
can't possibly go wrong.

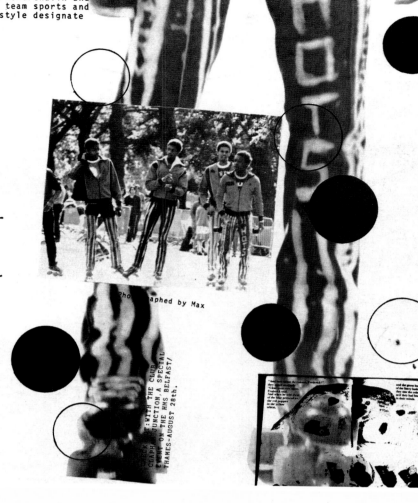

Photographed by Max

CRACK T:WITH THE CLUB
CHAPEL JUNCTION.A SPECIAL
EVENT ON THE HMS BELFAST/
THAMES-AUGUST 28th.

The scene on the stage

It all started with KLAUSS NOMI about a year ago,this outer space mime singing
operas in rock clubs,all decked out in his black tuxedo..
JOEY ARIA,his black singer,left him to create his own band,Strange Party,a combo
band gathering ten N.Y. cult figures.Staging,acting and real singing,make it one
of the newest type of visual act to catch.

Photographed by Michel Momy

artist will be very, very successful said a fortune teller.  MIKE ROBINSON
ts the romantic iconography we've been brought up with: couples kissing and
ting.
his dealer is the coolest in town.  BROOK ALEXANDER hangs out in the weirdest
s, looking for the new stuff.  Taking it out of the gutter, the white walls of
57th street gallery keeps inflation soaring and gives it an official stamp for
ulators.

The only genuine stage performer we have got here.
ALAN VEGA from suicide, oh man, you should see his tapes and his next solo album is
coming out soon and he is so sexy...
Just hold on, babe... it blows my mind, I have been doing the same shit for ten
years, man, and last week I played for 30 000 people in two nights.  Could not
believe it, man.  I was opening for the cars and man, they hated me, they started
throwing beer bottles at us, but shit, 30 000 guys.  And I had to meet all these
assholes of producers and promoters who all want to meet the stars, and I had to
shake hands and talk with these idiots.

70

YASMIN: Mode- Leather J'kt,£300 from Italy.Trousers ,£54.00 from Harrods."Way In'(Shoul-dn't it be called 'Way Out'?E.d.).Sloane Ranger goggles/Sunglasses,£12.00 from Paris-where else.Fav MusicJazz n;Steve Carr.Yasmin is studying knitwear at Middlesex Poly' and makes Pizzas for a part time job.(Must make a pile out a' Pizzas.E.d.)

PATRICE: Mode-J'kt n"T'rs £1.00 from a Jumble Sale,set of with Luftwaffe boots n'trilby. (Full marks for ingenuity.E.d.)Fav" Music PIL,Reggae n" Rock n'Roll.At present Patrice is looking for a job.........

"Wearing my suit-It is your character.There is a limit-over your shoulder.Everyone loves you until they know you.A few aerosols may champion a stranger.Standing around all the right people)...'Suit" on Metal Box album by PIL..............

"London Bridge Is Falling Down"

MEL and JOSS: Mode - Mel found everything she's wearing at jumble sales except the Dr Marten boots that cost £4 down Petticoat Lane. Unemployed, she lends a hand in her mother's pub. Fave music reggae and two-tone, on skinheads she says: "First time round, in the late '60's it was style and music that was all important. The skins I know these days are more interested in trouble when they get together.

Mode - Joss bought her jacket in Portobello Rd. Market, her Mum added the studs, including JOSS studded across the back for easy I.D.

MEL: Mode-"I've been in this J'kt for 10 y"rs.I had loads more badges,half get nicked a-nd half were lost in fights,but there yer go.The 1½ badge means all bikers have at least 1½ of bad in them,its our law."said he.His leather also boasts an Eddie Cochran badge-he loves rock n'roll, almost as much as his 750cc Triumph Bonnaville.....

I WAS WONDERING WHY YOU PUT D.H.LAWRENCE ?
CAUSE I LIKE HIM
IS HE YOUR FAVOURITE WRITER ?
YEAH
DID YOU PAINT THAT ON YOURSELF ?
YEAH
WHAT OTHER WRITERS DO YOU LIKE
NO-ONE
THAT'S IT ?
I LIKE JEAN PAUL SARTRE BUT HE'S NOTHING TO
D.H.LAWRENCE

LISTEN TO THIS...

extract from 'The Rainbow'by D.H.Lawrence.

Silently, obediently, she took off her hat and gave herself to his arms again. He liked her - he liked the feel of her - he wanted to know her more closely. He let his fingers subtly seek out her cheek and neck. What amazing beauty and pleasure, in the dark! His fingers had often touched Anna on the face and neck like that. What matter! It was one man who touched Anna, another who now touched this girl. He liked best his new self. He was given over altogether to the sensuous knowledge of this woman, and every moment he seemed to be touching absolute beauty, something beyond knowledge.

Very close, marvelling and exceedingly joyful in their discoveries, his hands pressed upon her, so subtly, so seekingly, so finely and desirously searching her out, that she too was almost swooning in the absolute of sensual knowledge. In utter sensual delight she clenched her knees, her thighs, her loins together!

It was an added beauty to him.

But he was patiently working for her relaxation, patiently, his whole being fixed in the smile of latent gratification, his whole body electric with a subtle, powerful, reducing force upon her. So he came at length to kiss her, and she was almost betrayed by his insidious kiss. Her open mouth was too helpless and unguarded. He knew this, and his first kiss was very gentle, and soft, and assuring, so assuring. So that her soft, defenceless mouth became assured, even bold, seeking upon his mouth. And he answered her gradually, gradually, his soft kiss sinking in softly, softly, but ever more heavily, more heavily yet, till it was too heavy for her to meet, and she began to sink under it. She was sinking, sinking, his smile of latent gratification was becoming more tense, he was sure of her. He let the whole force of his will sink upon her to sweep her away. But it was too great a shock for her. With a sudden horrible movement she ruptured the state that contained them both.

'Don't - don't!'

It was a rather horrible cry that seemed to come out of her, not to belong to her. It was some strange agony of terror crying out the words. There was something vibrating and beside herself in the noise. His nerves ripped like silk.

'What's the matter?' he said, as if calmly. 'What's the matter?'

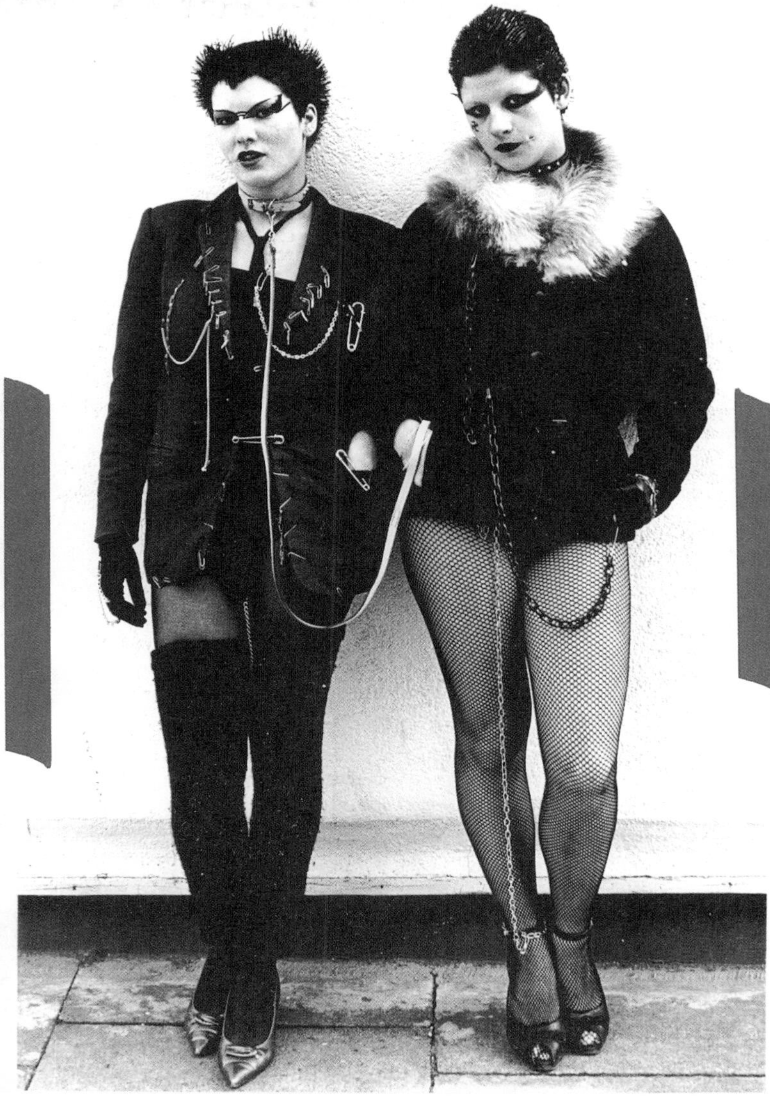

3

WiLD!

STRAIGHT UP

Photographed by Steve Johnston

COLIN: Mode - Colin is wearing black pleated trousers which he made himself. The cardigan is from Marks and Spencers, £9.99 and the shoes from Axiom in the Kings Road, £5.99. Fave music - Siouxsie and the Banshees and David Bowie.

Anonymous girl with spiky hair-do.

Clockwise: Spread from Not Another Punk Book, the original straight-up. ph. Steve Johnston   US issue ph. Christian Witkin   Fifteenth birthday issue October 1995 ph. Juergen Teller and Wolfgang Tillmans

photography by **christian witkin**
co-ordination by **andrew dosunmu**
thanks to kelton lab, color edge,
8 bond studio (all in new york city)
and mimi wlodarczyk

# BROADWAY CUTS THROUGH THE HEART OF NEW YORK CITY. WE SET UP A STUDIO THERE TO CAPTURE THE WILD INDIVIDUALISTS PASSING BY.

**Mickey Boardman**, 27, publisher's assistant and writer for *Paper* magazine. Clothes found on street, from flea markets, shoes from Polo Ralph Lauren. Favourite record: *Very Necessary* by Salt-N-Pepa. Loves: "The fun thing is having access to resources that allow you to produce your ideas from the street to the boutiques of twisted talented designers, you have a smorgasbord of ideas and inspirations to keep you excited!"

**Mary Iggy Frey**, 25, works for Liquid Sky. Clothes from Liquid sky, K-Mart and my dad. Sunglasses from the Glorious Clothing Company in London. Favourite records: *Jungle Sky* and *Freedom Is The Movement* by DJ Soulslinger. Loves: "Working my ass off, rollerblading, underground dance, UFOs, my dog Rabbi, New York fucking City, life itself, the passion to unite, rise above the bullshit government. Power to the people, friends, animals, Earth, aliens, the homeless, Africa and you!"

**Jill Nichols**, 29, sculptor. Wears secondhand jeans, shoes by Stéphane Kélian, boyfriend's socks, knickers from England, bra top by Elon of California. Favourite record: "No favourite record, just my mix tape with lots of gutteral music." Loves: "Sculpting!"

**Akin Adams**, 24, "medianaut, consciousness explorer, time traveller – in plainer English, lead vocalist and guitarist for SAM". Pants from workwear store, kaftan home-made. Favourite records: King Crimson's *Discipline*, Public Enemy's *Nation Of Millions*, Jimi Hendrix's *Kiss The Sky*, Bob Marley And The Wailers' *Soul Captives*, The Specials' *The Specials*. Loves: "Playing with SAM, advocating hemp industrialization, being alive in the yet-to-blossom '90s, surviving in New York City."

i-D THE US ISSUE

SIGNS OF THE TIMES... 1980 On the eve of a US tour, Joy Division frontman Ian Curtis hangs himself in his Macclesfield kitchen · Liverpool post-punk flourishes with debut LPs from Echo And The Bunnymen and The Teardrop Explodes · The Blitz Club and the Goodge Place squat scene begin in London, the denizens of which (Spandau Ballet, Steve Strange, Jeremy Healy, Boy George) creep virus-like into the charts, clubs and shops of the 1980's and beyond · Fame is unleashed upon the nation's cinemas, afflicting adolescent wardrobes with a plague of lavender leg-warmers and sawn-off sweatshirts · Sony's Walkman launches, much to the chagrin of parents, teachers and the like · David Bowie's last 'relevant' album, *Scary Monsters*, is released · Ska music and fashion dominate under the influence of The Specials, The Beat and Madness · *Sandinista* by The Clash weighs in as the first punk-rock treble LP · A generation mourns the 'assassination' of John Lennon, gunned down outside his flat by Mark David Chapman · The Buggles' *Video Killed The Radio Star* is the first clip to be shown on MTV · Leigh Bowery arrives in London and lands himself a job in Burger King: greater things are yet to come · Five pretty boys who hang out at Birmingham's Rum Runner club form a band, taking their name from Roger Vadim's 1967 space-porn epic *Barbarella*. Ladies and gentlemen, we give you Duran Duran ►

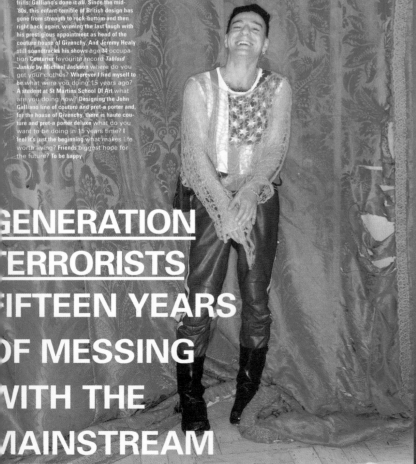

juergen teller

wolfgang tillmans

**JOHN GALLIANO** Bias-cut dresses, puff sleeves, tailored tinfoil jackets, flamenco frills: Galliano's done it all. Since the mid-'80s, this enfant-terrible of British design has gone from strength to rock-bottom and then right back again, winning the last laugh with his prestigious appointment as head of the couture house of Givenchy. And Jeremy Healy still soundtracks his shows age 34 occupation 'Couturier' favourite record *Tabloid Junkie* by Michael Jackson where do you get your clothes? Wherever I find myself to be what were you doing 15 years ago? A student at St Martins School Of Art what are you doing now? Designing the John Galliano line of couture and pret-a-porter and, for the house of Givenchy, there is haute couture and pret-a-porter deluxe what do you want to be doing in 15 years time? I feel it's just the beginning what makes life worth living? Friends biggest hope for the future? To be happy

# GENERATION TERRORISTS FIFTEEN YEARS OF MESSING WITH THE MAINSTREAM

**BLUR** Who do they think they are? Outwardly-mobile scruffs with a penchant for missing aitches, last album *Parklife* went straight to the top of the charts through a combination of swottiness, snottiness and unabashed love for the eclectic beast known as English culture. New magnum opus *The Great Escape* proves there's a lot more going on in their heads than gahn dahn the dogs. Hands-down winners in the Battle Of Britain name Damon Albarn age 27 occupation Singer/songwriter favourite record *Shaved Fish* by John Lennon and *It's Great When You're Straight... Yeah!* by Black Grape where do you get your clothes? Bankrupt stock and odd shops what were you doing 15 years ago? Starting comprehensive school what are you doing now? Having my picture taken what do you want to be doing in 15 years time? Not talking about what happened 15 years ago what makes life worth living? Tomorrow biggest hope for the future? To invent an alcoholic drink that doesn't have any side-effects once you've drunk it

Who says what you're going to wear tomorrow?

# Karl Lagerfeld

Spreads from Vanity Fair February 1971 ph. Frank Horvat, continued over leaf

# Karl Lagerfeld
## hiding behind the label 'Chloë'

**Bright, funny, he looks like a film star, and might have been born in the Seventies because his touch could surely not have come from any but a Martian age.**
He doesn't see women as romantic at all. 'We're not living in a romantic age,' he says simply. Instead, he's outrageous – his fabrics get shock treatment: bold, amusing, sophisticated, using clean sharp colours, breathtaking, larger-than-life prints straight off a canvas from Delaunay or Leger.
His energy fizzes over into designing shoes, furs, prints, knits, jewellery, hats, ties and scarves but **'I'm not a designer. Evolution is the designer. I merely follow.**
'I don't bear any age or type in mind when I work on a Collection, though' – with a grin – 'I definitely don't think one could say they're for the sporty, outdoor woman!'
You can't label Karl's collection, any more than you can the women surrounding him in his studio – actress/model/dancer Carol Labrié . . . Anna Piagi of Italian *Vogue* . . . or Donna Jordan, who, like Lagerfeld is acting in Warhol's film. They all share a secret quality, as if operating on a special wavelength of their own.

Details of all the clothes on page 79.

**You Might**

## Emmerton and Lambert lead this strong new
look – not just finding strange, old, beautifully made garments in fine fabrics, but developing a reaction against the humorless, production line garments in soul-less man-made fibres by remaking old fabrics into new clothes.
*Right now chenille table-cloths in age-softened colours,* art nouveau scarves and silk shawls are being combined into a collection of one-off garments as fascinating as they are individual.
Like the people who wear them.

Details of all the clothes on **page 79.**

# Mary Quant

**Irreverent . . . to extra-establishment eyes,**
iconoclastic . . . carelessly contemporary and *dans-le-vent*;
more than any other British
designer she has made whole
countries gasp with outrage and
reluctant admiration. Everyone
knows how dramatically Mary
skittled the staid old fuddy-duddy
fashion industry. That was
fifteen years ago. The
phenomenal thing is that she's
kept it up. She continues to
make news.

The girl
who put
paid to
prudery

A profile of MARY QUANT

*' A woman should
enjoy life to the full, be
ebullient, never afraid to experiment
with her looks. Her personality should
show through, she should be able to wear
any outfit at any time, just because it makes
her feel good. She mustn't be afraid to express
herself, she should never do anything in moderation.'*
Her collection this season is possibly her best yet. More than ever, her clothes breathe
freedom and vigour, have a positive attitude to contemporary living. The functional aspect
is apparent, clutter is anathema to her – one reason why her clothes correspond so completely 46▶

## Who says what you're going to wear tomorrow?

### Mary Quant

44◀ to today's demands and tempo. The sort of intelligent, fresh young women who
wear Mary's clothes find their prototype in someone like Lady Sarah Courage
the beautiful widow of the racing driver Piers Courage – it was she who modelled The
Quant Collection for Bonwit Teller in the US, she who Mary thinks
crystallises her consistently contemporary 'look'.

Details of all the clothes on page 79

47

'Most women have to rely on a husband for security'

'I don't envy the housewife stuck at home'

Crêpe de chine dress with flounced, wraparound skirt, £20 at Foale & Tuffin, 1 Marlborough Court, W1

Below satin jumpsuit by Radley, £5.75 at Originellp, Gloucester Road, SW7

45

If you're set on making money

# LOOK AS IF YOU'RE WORTH IT

Being poor but honest never got a girl anywhere – except stuck with the filing and treated to a half pint. People value you as much as you value yourself – which is another way of saying you have to dress rich to get rich. So here are some clothes to pull off the con trick. Crisply black and white, coolly elegant, and plainly destined to land you in the board room. With a glass of champers in your cheating hand of course.

Black cotton blazer and trousers, £9.95 and £4.95 at Stirling Cooper; voile shirt, £10.50 at James Drew, Burlington Arcade, W1V 9AB; belt 75p at Way In;

White blazer suit with black piping, £6.95 for the jacket, £4.50 for the trousers, at Stirling Cooper, 26 Wigmore Street, W1H 1LD; cotton jersey shirt, £2.25 from all branches of Dorothy Perkins. Striped patent belt £1.50 at Miss Selfridge, Duke Street, W1M 5DA; silk hat by George Malyard, £12.50 (with matching scarf) at Just Looking, Kings Road, SW3 4TZ. Fluorescent beads by Adrien Mann about 69p at John Lewis, Oxford Street, W1A 1EX.

44
45

One of my favourite issues of "Vanity Fair" was themed,
'who says what you're going to wear tomorrow?' Each designer's portrait was followed by a representation of their
collection reflecting their attitudes. This was followed by
another theme in 1972, 'the Woman's Liberation issue',
where all the women photographed chose their own clothes,
apart from a dozen models in wedding dresses! For "Vanity
Fair" the best issues were always created around a theme
which meant that the team of people working on the issue
had a common focus. "i-D" themes, from the very start, were
esoteric, fighting against people who had to put everything
into pigeon-holes. I would ask the visual contributors to
the magazine not to illustrate a word, but to capture a
feeling that fitted whatever our working title was. We have
continued this formula. It is never intended to restrict
editorial content, but helps give a visual thread to the
issue, whether it's travel, sex, escapism, technology or
talent. We are currently working on a project 'the most
influential people in fashion in the 90s'.
The working partnership with "i-D" photographers begins
with my request to pare the image down to a person against
a white wall. I'm always more interested in the subject
than the technique or the background and look for photographers who can get under the skin of an individual. The
technical effects and formats are a secondary ingredient,
but one which I'm still very fascinated by. I talk about
directions and feeling which I wish the magazine to move
towards, and let stylists and photographers develop their

own ideas, their own interpretations. There is no rational
approach to deciding which photographer is good for what,
it's totally about feeling.
With each issue I try to balance a graphic photographic
style with a documentary style, as the flow and pace of the
magazine is at its best where pages complement each other.
For most of the team the frustration is that they don't
have the whole picture, that's in my head and I'm constantly shuffling it around until the final deadline.
I first met Bob Richardson in 1972, at the "Vanity Fair"
office. The first words he said to me were, "What sign are
you, man". He shot Anjelica Houston for the rich-girl cover
and story. Year's later, when I heard he was going to be in
Milan I asked him to do a story for "i-D" which he shot in
his hotel with model,Iris Palmer stylist Christine Fortune,
and an Italian that she met on the street. His son, Terry
Richardson, was already a frequent contributor to "i-D" but
that is no surprise given the "mafia" nature of this business!
Anjelica Houston also featured on one of my favourite
"Vogue" covers a few years later. Bailey, working with
Manolo Blahnik, photographed the first full-length British
"Vogue" cover which did record sales in its first week.

photography by **terry richardson**

Bridget, 24, singer with NYC Loose

Unknown doorman at Brownies club

# 2.15
## ON AVENUE A

Late at night, hanging out with New York's rock'n'roll underground

# VOGUE

JAN
35p

happy looks –
what you'll be
wearing . . .
clothes,
make-up,
hair, health,
all that's newest
and brightest

happy days –
what and who's
happening . . .
good times ahead

happy travelling –
where you'll
be going . . .

## HAPPY NEW YEAR

Clockwise: Spread from i-D spread Pin-up issue ph. David Bailey   British Vogue cover January 1973 ph. Bob Richardson   i-D No. 165 June 1997 ph. Terry Richardson

"You have to take a positive line, if you work only with the negative side it becomes destructive.

You can generate the energy or tap into it - I work to create energy".

"You have to take a positive line. You can generate the energy or tap into it. I work to create energy and prefer to ad lib on the deadline. Lateral thinkers are essential, telepathic lateral thinkers get the job."

We had built up a trusting, working relationship with Willy Bogner on a couple of projects apart from his Fire and Ice clothing collection. I re-cut a TV commercial using footage cut to a John Lee Hooker blues track, "Shake It Baby". I also compiled and edited a book on the story of "White Magic - the Movie", which was like an album. Willy liked the energetic approach to the stuff that I been doing for Fire and Ice and in particular the photographic direction. It's a style which is meant to look easy but is hard to achieve. He commissioned me to direct a fashion shoot in Majorca and asked Tricia to produce it. I chose to work with photographer Donald Christie. I wanted to do action pictures on 5x4 - something I never tried before. But having worked with Donald at "i-D", I knew he was the person I could trust to get results. The concept was people and movement, with a sophisticated graphic image. Fire and Ice became a client when I was approached by the Munich based ad agency Start to give them some creative direction for their young sportswear client. Tricia and I were invited to Munich, to a shoot for the 92 winter collection. I had suggested that Wolfgang Tillmans, who was still a photography student, come along to take portraits of the snowboarders to contrast the work of two sports-

action photographers. The shoot was chaos with hair and make-up, it was clear that they lacked direction and I ended up art directing and later in the day discovered that had always been Greg's intention. I did the best I could, and laid the stuff out. That was the start of my collaboration with Willy Bogner, Fire and Ice and Start. Then I was taken on as art director of the entire campaign. At that time Fire and Ice had already established the idea of a "tribe" which I wanted to expand, taking the concept one stage further with a nomadic tribe exploring the globe. We dispensed with hairdressers, make-up artists and stylists. The idea was to do some careful casting - all the models were non-models - and give them the experience of a lifetime. Our first "Real Life Adventure" was to Namibia, with the greatest sand-dunes on earth. I had to direct television spots, an ad campaign and a catalogue. Namibia was an important trip for me. The place had a very special feeling that I had never experienced anywhere else before. I was working with three photographers, Thomas Kalak, Steffen Gentis and Uli Wiesmeier. Steffen, the main photographer, had grown up in South Africa and knew Namibia well. After the first two days the clothes still looked too clean, too like a regular fashion shoot. I suggested to Marco Lauer, the client, that we wash everything in a river and lay it all out to dry in the sun. I knew I had a very special client when he let us drive 4WD's across the entire collection!

BOGNER

spring/summer '97

Willy Bogner GmbH & Co. KGaA., Sankt-Veit-Straße 4  81673 München  Tel. (089) 43606.0
Photos by Donald Christie, Directed by Terry Jones. Printed in Germany

Spreads from Willy Bogner catalogue spring/summer 1997 ph. Donald Christie

joy

balance

speed

harmony

FIRE
& ICE
SPRING/SUMMER '93

Snakes
have
right
of
way

TRY OR DIE!

Willy Bogner  Namibia Fire and Ice ad. spring/summer 1993 ph. Uli Wiesmeier   Iceland Fire and Ice winter 1994 ph. Stefan Ruiz

ride th

FIRE

With Fire and Ice the idea was to maximise the potential of
a situation which was more an adventure than your run-of-
the-mill fashion shoot. There were no four star hotels just
log cabins or tents, outside toilets, plenty of fresh air,
kids who'd answered an ad, and a big bag of clothes. I
wanted to bring a new energy into photography, and a style
began to evolve. For the second trip, to Alaska, I chose to
work with Stefan Ruiz, a photographer from San Franscico
who had already worked for "i-D". I also took along
Dominique Lutier, who had edited some of the recent "i-D
mashes". As a cameraman he recorded the trips on film and
video as well as in stills.
After Namibia, Tricia and I agreed that she would accompany
me on the next trip as assistant producer. Fire and Ice
became my major client and our year was divided into bi-
annual trips, one autumn/winter shoot in May, with the
spring/ summer shoot in October. In between each adventure
the catalogue had to be produced, and we made TV spots from
the footage we'd shot which ran as fifteen-second slots on
MTV Europe. Fire and Ice was the ideal client. We had the
trust and support of the managing director, Marco Lauer,
and the company director, Willy Bogner, gave us his creative backing.
The concept of the tribe grew as we travelled through
Alaska, Hawaii, Iceland, Australia, USA, Canada. We learnt
from mistakes and built on successes. We developed a formula for the best results - and as Freyr Jakobson, our
Icelandic guide and friend would say - "no problem!".

crater

&ICE

Where the hell is Chit'na?

FIRE&ICE

WILLY BOGNER PRESENTS FIRE & ICE CLOTHING COMPANY

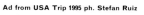

**Ad from USA Trip 1995 ph. Stefan Ruiz**
Steve Klassen, world champion snowboarder, was picking up rubbish from the site that overlooked Monument Valley. As a US citizen he was embarrassed by all the litter that had been dumped in such a beautiful position but his face, when he found the dollar note, produced the portrait that made the ad.
**Chris Carr in Iceland video still by Dominique Lutier ph. Stefan Ruiz**
Each journey was punctuated with many pit stops and photo opportunities which Stefan would cover on panoramic and square formats that I could cut to wide shots. The partnership with Stefan produced some great images.

"ON THE BOARD: IT'S AN EXTENSION OF YOU, THE STYLE YOU RIDE IS AN EXTENSION OF YOU." CHRIS

"I THOUGHT IT WAS BEAUTIFUL - YEAH - ONE OF THE MOST BEAUTIFUL SUNSETS I'VE EVER SEEN." REUBEN

FACT: In 1959, Hawaii became the 50th state in the United States of America.

FACT: The Hawaiian islands are the most isolated in the world, geographically as far as you can get from Earth's continents.

"STARS ARE HOLES IN THE VEIL AND I'M LOOKING INTO THE BRIGHTNESS OF ANOTHER WORLD."

**FACT:** At the top of the mountain the air feels incredibly clean, so clean that you feel your head is bursting.

Pages from Fire and Ice catalogue Hawaii spring/summer 1994 ph. **Stefan Ruiz**

# WANTED

**THIS IS AMBER, ONE OF EIGHT INTREPID SNOWBOARDER WHO JOINED THE FIRE & ICE PHOTO-SHOOT IN ICELAN LAST YEAR.** We're planning our next trip and looking for guys and gi (aged 20+). Can you board on snow, on tarmac or on wate Can you dive into lagoons and come up smiling? Can you ride for hours wi out getting saddle sore? Live under the skin of people you've never met befor Put out for the cameras 24 hours a day? Are you energised enough to keep going? one thing's for sure, you've got to be more than just a pretty fa

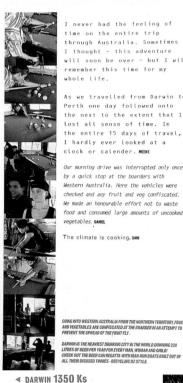

I never had the feeling of time on the entire trip through Australia. Sometimes I thought – this adventure will soon be over – but I will remember this time for my whole life.

As we travelled from Darwin to Perth one day followed onto the next to the extent that I lost all sense of time. In the entire 15 days of travel, I hardly ever looked at a clock or calender. MEEKE

*Our morning drive was interrupted only once by a quick stop at the boarders with Western Australia. Here the vehicles were checked and any fruit and veg confiscated. We made an honourable effort not to waste food and consumed large amounts of uncooked vegetables.* DANIEL

*The climate is cooking.* DANI

COING INTO WESTERN AUSTRALIA FROM THE NORTHERN TERRITORY, FRUIT AND VEGETABLES ARE CONFISCATED AT THE BOARDER IN AN ATTEMPT TO PREVENT THE SPREAD OF THE FRUIT FLY.

DARWIN IS THE HEAVIEST DRINKING CITY IN THE WORLD DOWNING 230 LITRES OF BEER PER YEAR FOR EVERY MAN, WOMAN AND CHILD! CHECK OUT THE BEER CAN REGATTA WITH MAN-RUN BOATS BUILT OUT OF ALL THEIR DISUSED TINNIES - RECYCLING OZ STYLE.

◄ DARWIN 1350 Ks

Just to add a bit more juice to our 'boring' trip we spotted a 12ft rock python. Adam, 'the Nutter', jumps two ledges, runs head level in front of this so ugly beast, grabs it and holds it above his head like some Tarzan warrior, but not before it chomps his hand three times. Nope it's not over. Then it begins to strangle him, his eyes almost pop before he releases its hold and it's all over. The snake lives and Adam lives. I had nothing to comment on for a long time after seeing Adam and the snake doing it. My admiration and respect to all who participated! DANI

Camp at the waterfall. Most of the day we carried all our stuff up this hill. As we arrived at the top - amazing! The view was like the best assorted chocolate my eyes could ever get. This was my paradise valley. Everything was there - vegetation, a crocodile that swam in the small pool beneath us. Before we could turn around, the big snake appeared. Adam turned into a real Dundee. The snake and Adam started to fight. Dundee got bitten. But thank God it was not a poisonous one. We just all waited there with our mouths and eyes open... this was real. We even had this snake in our hands, all of us. The skin was soft and I could feel the muscle inside. ELLY

Fire and Ice Canada Story 1996/97 ph. Stefan Ruiz    Ad Fire and Ice Iceland Story 1994/95

# FIRE&ICE

WILLY BOGNER PRESENTS FIRE & ICE CLOTHING COMPANY

*"IT'S A LITTLE LIKE THE GAME OF LIFE: GETTING DOWN A MOUNTAIN AND DOING IT THE BEST WAY. THERE'S HUNDREDS OF WAYS OF GETTING OFF A MOUNTAIN AND YOU TRY TO FIND YOUR WAY, YOU HAVE TO TRUST IN YOURSELF..."* RETO

Fire & Ice: USA Story. Escape from Vegas

STEVE: A global experience – I don't think that there's anything else out there like this, bringing people together in sport who are all from different places and have different personalities. Everyone is able to look beyond everybodys' weird, quirky personality and accept each other, it's really cool. It's a good learning experience.

Fire and Ice USA Story 1995: We had the idea to fly into Las Vegas, drive to the Colorado mountains and return via the Moab desert. I had seen snow on the La Sal mountain when Tricia and I had planned our trip the month before. I had a definite picture in my mind for the cover and as we drove to Moab from Telluride I hoped there would be enough snow for Reto Lamm to flip his snowboard as the sun was setting over the desert. With Stefan and Reto we rode up a track in the mountain until we got the view. Pure chance! Had to happen...

**VERENA:** Es gibt Menschen, die schmeißen eben alles hin. So einen hab ich am Lake Powell getroffen, ein Weltenbummler mit einem uralten VW-Bus. Wir sind erst nach einer halben Stunde draufgekommen, daß wir beide aus Österreich sind! Ich bin auf das Bus-Dach geklettert und hab dort oben meine Karotte (und gleichzeitig mein Mittagessen) gelassen - einziger Trost:

meine Karotte fährt
jetzt acht Monate quer
durch die USA, wer
weiß, vielleicht auch
noch länger.

"THE OCEAN IS A BEAUTIFUL THING THAT WE ARE KILLING WITH ALL OF OUR HUMAN EXCREATIONS." REUBEN

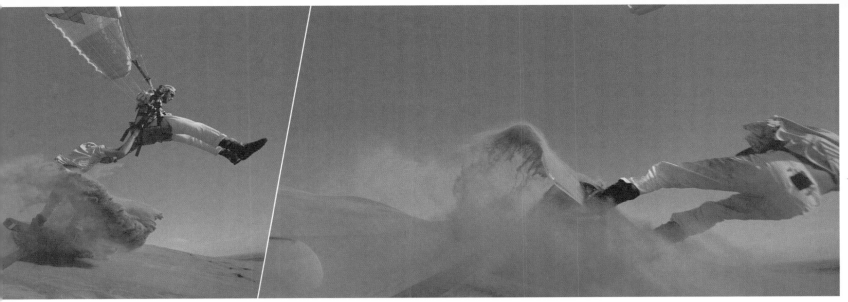

Fire and Ice catalogue Namibia Story summer 1993, in the double gatefold ph. Steffan Gentis and Uli Wiesmeier    Hawaii  Story, towards the sea catalogue, summer 1994  ph. Stefan Ruiz and Thomas Kalak

MMING WITH A SPECIES THAT'S MILLIONS OF YEARS OLD. TRYING TO SWIM GRACEFUL LIKE THEM. TRYING NOT TO SPOOK THEM. I DIDN'T TOUCH THEM. YOU CAN'T TOUCH THEM,
FEDERAL OFFENCE. PEOPLE WANT TO KILL THEM FOR THEIR EGGS AND SHELLS. TOUCHING THEM IS INVADING THEIR SPACE. YOU DON'T GO INTO SOMEONE'S HOUSE,
THEM, JUMP ON THEIR BACK AND SAY 'LET'S GO FOR A JOY RIDE!'" REUBEN

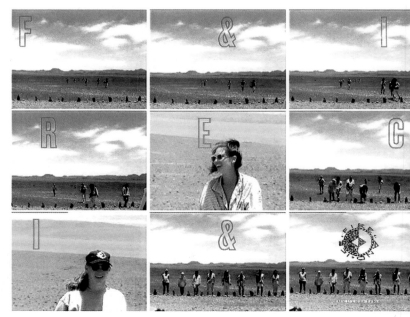

**OPEN YOUR EYES-LOOK BEYOND WHAT YOU CAN SEE**

Fire and Ice winter 1993/94 Alaska portfolio, based on the six senses ph. Stefan Ruiz, Thomas Kalak and Vianney Tisseau

TV spots for Fire and Ice, filmed in Namibia 1993

Graphics for Rapido TV special "Rock in the 80s". Low budget annimation, using jump cuts with Apple Mac low resolution typography 1989, before the days of the Power Mac and cheap digital editing

sexe, drogue et rock'n'roll

techno

madonna

madonna

104

Most of the television work I've done has its origin in
print. The advantage with television is that you can add
movement and graphic sound. My interest in video and television graphics was fuelled by that massive potential. Some
ideas were never resolved, we didn't have the time. Some
were resolved by other people with commercial budgets.
Editing "on the fly" became an art form. Armed with a car-
rier bag of new sounds, recommended by "i-D" staff, and
whatever video tapes I could grab from my studio, one
"mash" was simply added to the one before. "video mash 1",
was edited with George Barber, a friend of Dylan Jones,
then editor of "i-D". "Video Rex" was my first video-maga-
zine in 1986, produced for Wave with Shikita Kioshi, and
with a group of video artists working in London. The final
edit was produced on a VHS machine at Edit Video which John
Mayes had just set up.

John Mayes became my main collaborator on video projects,
from "i-D mashes" to Fire and Ice commercials, most of
which appeared really wild when shown on a stand in Olympia
during London Fashion Week. Designing for television, I
applied the magazine style to youth programmes "Reportage"
and "01 for London". Video-editing suites are equipped with
fantastic technology, but it's only ever as useful as the
technicians who operate it. I designed a tv identity which
could be put together weekly by Ian Bates and the graphics
studio in Manchester. Using the Paintbox system, we frame-
grabbed replayed video footage, enlarged the pixels and
changed the colours.

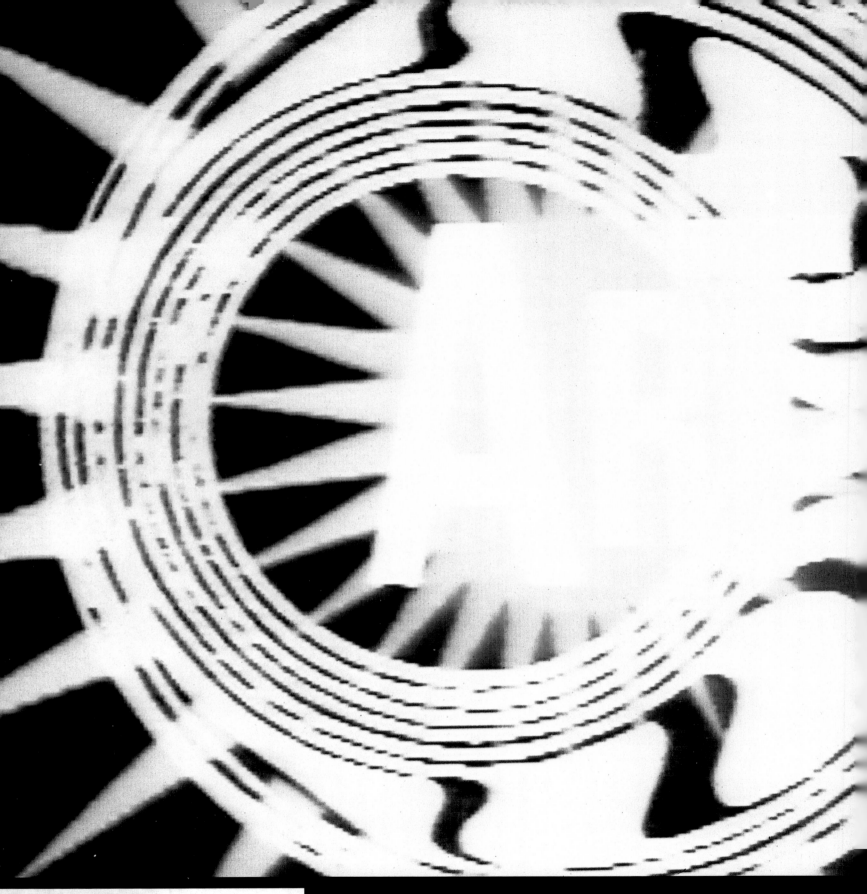

In 1987 I had been working on an idea for i-D TV with Mark Lebon and Crunch Productions. A producer contacted me to make a weekly events programme that became "01 for London". I designed the logo and my first TV graphic for Tom Gutteridge.

01- for London

"Reportage" was a programme for BBC2. I produced the logo and type style with the art department in Manchester. The title sequence was made using the logo as a stencil with rotating letters. This processed sequence played back with the headlining item, giving the programmes a punchy graphic identity way outside conventional television formulas. At Superchannel, I wanted to create an identity for the station without using words or a narrative structure, as it broadcast across seventeen countries. The Superchannel programme ident was produced for Tim Newman of Rapido TV in 1988. I produced low budget graphic mashes combined with moving type layer, with a different colour combination for each day.

1988 i-D Mash Tokyo

1993 Levis i-D Now exhibition London

1987 i-D Mash

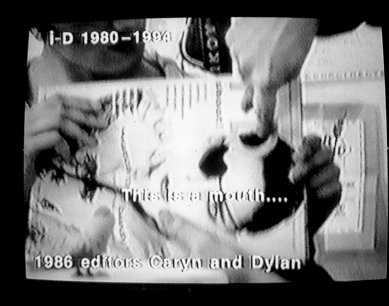

This is a mouth....

1986 editors Caryn and Dylan

1992 i-D Now exhibition Florence

1992 i-D Now exhibition Florence

1992 i-D Mash from Clothes Show Live

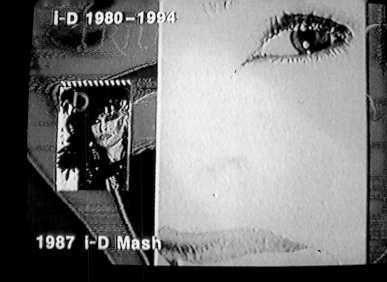

1987 i-D Mash

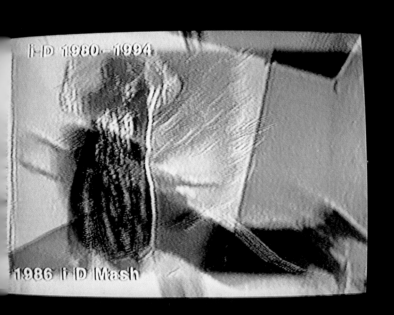

1986 i-D Mash

1990 i-D Mash

1988 i-D Mash Tokyo

1988 i-D Mash Tokyo

Polaroid from cover try for Sportswear International Ibiza 1979 ph. Carlo Orsi   Polaroid, with stylist Hamburg 1978 ph. Chico Bialas

110

My first client in Germany was "Sportswear International".
The publisher wanted a concept for a trade magazine to
attract the growing fashion sportswear market. Myself and
Toscani were bought in to work on the pilot issue. We met
in Nice and he produced twenty-four shots in twenty-four
hours, half the time we'd been booked. Toscani almost
killed the client when he tried to pay the model and stylist only half the agreed rate, but we were still asked to
produce issue one. On the third day, in freezing condi-
tions, photographing winter wear the styling co-ordinator
said, "oh by the way we have to shoot some bikinis and tennis clothes." The only solution was to do them on ice. Our
two Italian male models were supported around the rink by
the girl in the bikini. While she was dragging them around,
the pencil thin straps of her bikini broke - much to the
amusement of the watching crowd! I produced each issue
within a week, tracing off the photographs in my hotel room
in Düsseldorf. Chico Bialas was the Hamburg-based photographer they chose for the second issue. We shot the next two
issues on the streets of Hamburg, designing the layouts
while we were shooting. Chico took a number nine from a car
showroom which his wife Linda, who was a stylist, customised onto my jacket and said, if there's anything I
don't like I should point to this '9', nein meaning 'no'!
For a cover we had to photograph some boring jackets. To
the models' suprise, the cover shot was made when Chico and
I conspired to drench them with a bucket of water. The
client who paid for the cover credit was not amused.

## Warum mit den Reizen geizen?

*Ski-Urlaub ist ein Aktiv-Urlaub. Und nach dem Vergnügen auf den Pisten ist die sportliche Betätigung vielfach noch nicht beendet. Der Gang in die Sauna oder ins Schwimmbad ist bei vielen Skifans das Danach vor dem Trubel des abend- bis nächtlichen Après-Skis. Aber auch ein abendliches Treffen auf der Eislaufbahn bietet in richtigen Fitness- oder Trimm-Dich-Ferien die sportliche Abwechslung.*
*Ob der knappe Bikini der richtige Eislaufdress ist? Für „Otto Normalverbraucher" sicherlich nicht. Dennoch ein hübscher Vorschlag für das Bad im Hotel-Pool oder für Badeurlauber unter südlicher Sonne im Winter. Elemar. Daunenjacke: Castelbajac. Schal, Mütze, Handschuhe: Fiorucci. Strümpfe: Küffe.*

*Warum mit den Reizen geizen, wenn man eine makellose Bikini-Figur hat. Sie kann man mit einem kessen Tanga-Bikini gut zur Geltung bringen. Keusch verhüllend ist dagegen die Bermuda für Ihn, bedruckt mit einem Rankenmotiv. Alle Modelle: Elemar.*

Spread from Sportswear International Magazine Issue No.1 ph. Toscani Kirstie, sitting on the ice, wearing the bikini later became Toscani's wife

83

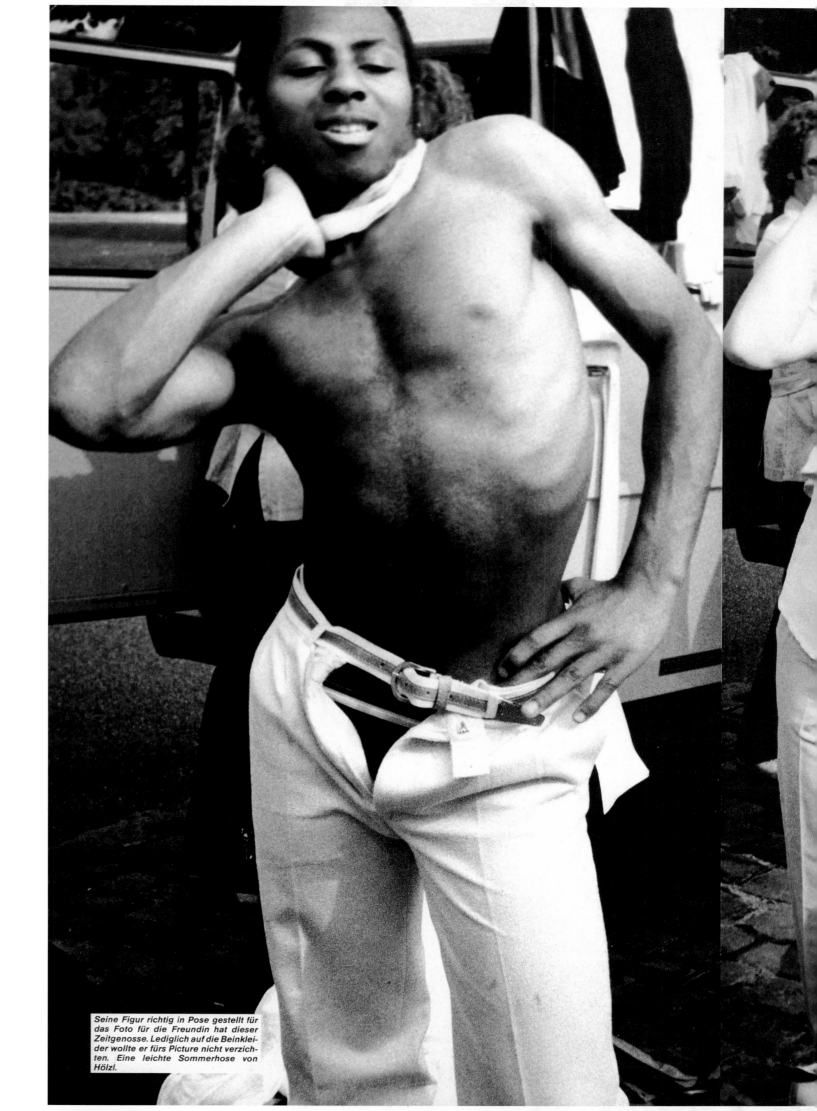

114

Seine Figur richtig in Pose gestellt für das Foto für die Freundin hat dieser Zeitgenosse. Lediglich auf die Beinkleider wollte er fürs Picture nicht verzichten. Eine leichte Sommerhose von Hölzl.

Spread from Sportswear International Issue No. 2 ph. Chico Bialas in Hamburg. We had so many clothes to photograph that day, so we decided to keep filming while having a picnic lunch in the middle of Hamburg.

Cordbesatz an Kragen und Revers setzt bei diesem weiten Hemd, das auch gut als Overshirt über Pullis und T-Shirts zu tragen ist, den Halsausschnitt richtig in Szene. Einhorn. Aus einer hochwertigen Flanellware die Tuchhose mit nicht auftragenden Bundfalten und Paspeltaschen. Koenen.

Leinenoptiken halten auch in der Hemdenmode ihren Einzug. Und aus einem solchen Warentyp ist das Sporthemd mit kleinem kurzem Reverskragen und plakativ aufgesetzter Brusttasche. Hatico. Zur gröberen Struktur des Leinens harmoniert gut das feine und fast glatte Oberflächenbild der Popeline-Hose. Hela.

Polo-Shirts kommen im bevorstehenden Sommer nicht nur in glatten Gewirken. So ist dieses Beispiel aus einer luftigen Netzmasche. Die Farbe: Ein vielseitig variierbares Olivgrün. Jacky Peer/Heinzelmann. In gerader Silhouette die Leinenhose von Hölzl. Gürtel: Dieter Spiess.

Damit auch die Frisur auf dem Foto tadellos sitzt, noch einmal schnell durchs Haar. Er wollte sich im Familienalbum sehen mit einem Overshirt aus transparentem Drehergewebe, das mit Schlupfausschnitt und ohne Kragen gearbeitet ist. Passend dazu der Schal. Lincron. Aus Popeline die Hose. Paas.

### Tweeds sind wieder auf dem Vormarsch

Tweedige Qualitäten, sei es gewebt oder gestrickt, ziehen in ihrer Bedeutung für den bevorstehenden Winter merklich an.
Tweed-Aspekte an V-Einsatz und Bund zeigt der Pullover mit betont dickem Rollkragen. dolores. Entsprechend dazu die Tweedhose. Berri.

### Überschnittene Schultern

Westover und Gilets gehören unbedingt in Sportswear-Sortimente, besonders wenn sie sich in eine legere Silhouette präsentieren und vielseitig zu kombinieren sind.
Durch eine stark überschnittene Schulterlinie fällt der Westover aus tweedigem Gestrick auf, zu dem die Bluse in dezenter Karo-Musterung gehört. joke + fun. Bundfalten à la Gatsby zeigt die Flanellhose. création michèle/leksens.

Westen, auch mit Plüsch-Innenleben oder -Abseite, trägt man im kommenden Winter nicht mehr nur unter, sondern auch über Jacken und Mänteln. Sie dürfen dabei in gleicher, aber auch in Kontrastfarbe gehalten sein. Weste mit Cord-Innenseite und Jacke sind von Marshal. Pulli: Marc O'Polo. Strickhütchen: Comte de Florence.

In Nesseloptik, wattiert und travers- und längsgesteppt, präsentiert sich die gut hüftlange Jacke mit Leder-Imitat-Besatz und praktischen Reißverschlußtaschen. Sie verlangt in ihrer neutralen Farbe nach ausdrucksvollen und farbfrischen Chosen. Modell: Hohenstein. Mütze, Pulli und Schal: Fiorucci.

18

*Zur Five-Pocket-Jeans aus Feincord bringt 49R ein Hemd in Melange-Musterung mit kleinem Kragen und weiten, ellbogenlangen Ärmeln.*

*Marshal*
*Figurbetonung ist vor allem bei schlanken jungen Mädchen wieder gefragt.*

*In frischen und fröhlichen Sommerfarben der Taille durch einen Tunnelgürtel verstellbar die beiden Hosenanzüge, der durch eine bar. Reihe ideenreicher Details belebt werden. Beim rotgelben Anzug bilden die tiefliegende Das grün/weiße Modell wird mit weißen tergezogene gelbe Passe und die gestreif-Druckknöpfen geschlossen. Die Hose ist in fen Strickbündchen den Blickfang. Schuhe: Arche und Otter.*
*Seitennaht ist die in der Länge etwas verkürzte Damenjeans, zu der Marshal ein Knalleng und mit Paspel und Schlitz in der T-Shirt mit Nummer à la Sporttricot assortiert.*

*49R*
*Jeans und Tops aus einer Hand – das erspart das langwierige und oft vergebliche Suchen nach dem exakt passenden Farben. Farblich abgestimmt ist das Kurzarm-Hemd mit mehrfarbigem Karo auf die Baumwollsatin-Hose mit interessanter Vorderteschenklösung. Kombinationen wirken besonders sportlich und passen gut zum klassischen Jeansanzug.*

On a subsequent photo shoot in Ibiza with the Italian photographer Carlo Orsi, I was told, under no circumstance get
the clothes wet! We had to shoot a pair of bright red jeans
and a yellow t-shirt. To keep the colours primary I needed
a swimming pool. A friend of Carlo's had the best pool on
the island and a blue inflatable dingy. We told both models
to get into the dingy very carefully...we didn't tell them
they were going to have to stand up when they got to the
middle of the pool, and still stay dry! Need less to say
the client was no happy and we were instructed to re-shoot
in Berlin. I next worked with Chico for the Dutch manufac-
turer Moustache and Emmanuelle who wanted me to come up
with a new name and a new image for their clothing company.
I suggested ME x (kiss) x (kiss). Each Mexx catalogue was
made like a magazine, themed around a different city and I
used "i-D" journalists to do the words.
My design attitude is to channel energy, to produce a message by impulse and intuition. My work is to communicate,
using whatever resources I have to hand at the time - old
and new methods - using technology without the restriction
of understanding how it works. Then you can react to spon-
taneous, controlled accidents while in search of momentary,
perfect solutions. My role is to conceive ideas, and
through interaction with people who have specific skills,
with technology and very little time, to produce images for
magazines, television or any other media.
When I began art directing, at "Vanity Fair", I treated it
as if I was making a film, often working with one main pho-

tographer. That was difficult to do at "Vogue", because
each of the fashion editors was keen to defend their pages.
"i-D" is diverse, because of the personalities of its contributors, so it reflects the individuality of expression,
in both words and pictures. My job is to keep the magazine
on one philosophical track. That's how the attitude of the
magazine has stayed constantly irreverent and occasionally
- or perhaps frequently - experimental.
Dylan Jones, group editor for "Arena" and "The Face":
"Terry is one of the most perverse people I've ever worked
with, a genuine maverick with a wicked sense of mischief
and a healthy disrespect for the medium at hand. A true
lateral thinker, he is a champion of juxtaposition and a
custodian of the absurd....if Terry were asked to redesign
the traffic light he'd make all three colours green... At
'i-D' he taught me the art of exploiting everything but the
obvious, but I've still not come to terms with his almost
total disrespect for the written word. My first experience
of Terry's subbing abilities involved him tearing off the
last six inches of a piece because it wouldn't fit though I
am slowly beginning to see his point."

Photography by David Lasnett
Model: Stella Tennant at Select

*DIFFERENT, MODERN, ORIGINAL, INVIGORATING, PURE, UNCONVENTIONAL, RAW. THAT'S THE DICTIONARY DEFINITION - BUT WHAT EXACTLY DOES FRESH MEAN? MORE IMPORTANTLY, WHAT DOES IT MEAN IN STYLE TERMS THIS SUMMER? WE INVITED TEN PHOTOGRAPHERS TO INTERPRET THE IDEA FOR A SPECIAL PORTFOLIO; THE FOLLOWING PAGES DOCUMENT THEIR RESPONSES, A SHARED SPIRIT OF HEALTH, FITNESS AND VITALITY. THE FREEWHEELIN' FEELING STARTS HERE...*

# fresh n up!

Two thirds of the earth's surface is covered in it, 65 percent of the human body is made from it, it can kill you and yet you can't live without it. It is, of course, water. In the last decade, this essential element has had marketing men wetting themselves with excitement as they find 'new' sources (like we don't really know that it's just fallen rain), repackage them and then see how much they can charge. Latest development comes from hip Paris boutique Colette, who actually have a water bar in their cafe with a menu that offers no less than 48 different varieties. And the most popular? Perhaps unsurprisingly, the ones with the best shaped bottles...
1. 'Water of the day' (this is changed daily)
2. Wattwiller (shaped like a vodka bottle)
3. Quarzia (quartz design bottle)

Shot at Colette, 213 Rue Saint Honore, Paris 75001

Photography by Michel Momy
Assisted by Patrick Anin
Styling by Miriam Roesri
Hair by Stephane Lancien at JL David
Make-up by Delphive Ehrard
Model: Shiraz at City

## wet 'n' wild

# clarity

Photography by Steven Klein
Styling by Edward Enninful
Hair by Gavin for John Frieda Salon

Photography by Matt Jones
Styling by Vanina Sorrenti
Hair by Zaiya at Susan Price Inc
Make-up by Shally at Streeters
Model: Lola Schnabel

Lola wears dress by Ghost from
13-14 Hinde Street, London W1.

# purity

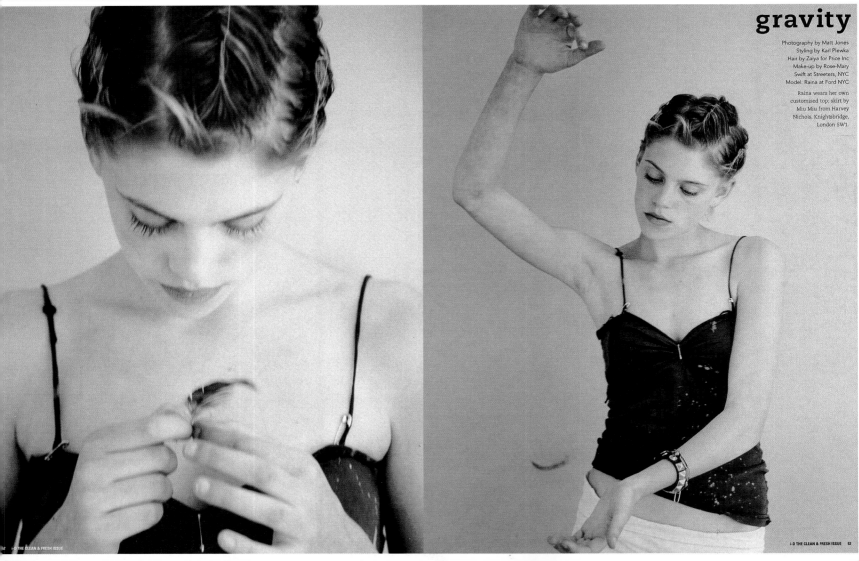

# gravity

Photography by Matt Jones
Styling by Karl Plewka
Hair by Zaiya for Price Inc
Make-up by Rose-Mary
Swift at Streeters, NYC
Model: Raina at Ford NYC

Raina wears her own
customised top; skirt by
Miu Miu from Harvey
Nichols, Knightsbridge,
London SW1.

JETZT

"Wenn ich ein Restaurant hätte, würde ich eine Frau einstellen, die nur dasitzt und so was anhat!" Das sagt Anthony Price, Englands phantasievollster Designer, zu seinen Entwürfen auf dieser Seite. Unten: Trägerloses Kleid aus rotem Seidentaft, Jacke aus grünem Seidentaft mit spiralenförmiger Krause vom Nacken bis zu den Handgelenken. Oben: Kleid aus Seidentaft (schwarz-, pink- und purpurfarben). Die riesige Rückenschleife ersetzt den Gürtel.

Zeigen Sie selbst mal, was Mode ist! Die Macher sind uneins — das ist Ihre Stunde! Tragen Sie Seide im Supermarkt und Kühnes im Konzert, Pailletten auf der Post und Dramatisches beim Derby — Mode ist, was Ihnen gefällt! VOGUE gibt auf vielen Seiten Anregungen und Tips.

# WAGEN SIE'S

Make-up: Patti Burris für Elizabeth Arden; Haare: Simon of Schumi, London.

Neil Kirk

56

57

Instant is an illusion. An instant is a frozen image in the space of a lifetime. Instant Design is a tiny graphics studio based in north London. Instant Design is a world-wide graphic design consultancy operating in Britain, Germany, France, Italy, the USA and Japan. Instant Design has generated a huge body of work which is always recognisable and always changing; which borrows from a wide range of influences, from Russian Constructivists to Op and Pop Art, and which has itself been looted by other designers. Instant design is a vocabulary, a collection of techniques which allows for design systems which have almost nothing in common with conventional grids and rules. The results give the illusion of speed, but the final artwork may or may not have been made speedily. Many of the instant design techniques produce graphics which look disordered but which also repay close reading. Instant design techniques go beyond the boundaries of graphic design, by using old typewriters and handwriting, by highlighting the process of making graphics, by playing with photocopies and Polaroids. Or they're graphic processes taken to the extreme, so as to defy conventions, such as legibility. Instant design leaves room for accidents.

For more than half my professional working life I've been publishing "i-D". What began as a diversion to commercial work is now a business which still sustains its original concept - to be an alternative voice giving editorial space to new ideas and people with innovative views. During the mid-90s, I gave increased freedom to the editorial staff to choose the magazine's direction. But after a few years with more of a music bias, I decided to steer the magazine back to the core concept, as a fashion forum with a broad vision.

Photography is the quickest way to show an idea. And the photographers who regularly contribute to "i-D" are encouraged to put passion into the work they produce for us. Over the years that passion has sometimes led to friction, even arguments. When a disagreement happens with a photographer who I want to continue working with, we usually manage to find a solution. There has to be mutual respect between the magazine - or rather myself as art director - and the photographer. I like the photographer to make their choices first, and often involve them in the process of design but I always put the dynamic of the magazine first. Sometimes taking chances and experimenting with graphics is more in the interest of the magazine as a whole than the personal interest of a photographer. I often have to explain the idea of "healthy irreverence" to a contributor who feels that their photos haven't been given enough respect. Photographers must trust what's best for the magazine. That's where the idea of mutual respect comes in. However, running bars of type across photos, chopping off heads, scalpel cut-outs, cartoon bubbles, blocks of overlayed colour, are just some of my 'crimes' which got me into trouble as early as "Vogue", back in the 70s.

**Perlen, Pailletten, Samt und Seide, raffiniert geschnittene Kleider, die Ihre Affären umschmeicheln - bei Cocktail, Dinner und zärtlichen Momenten. Für Mutige: Pailletten dürfen auch noch frühmorgens glänzen!**

<u>Links:</u> Die Verführung. Nachtschwarzes Crêpe-de-Chine-Kleid (Seide von Abraham) mit * Spitzenärmeln. Hochgeschlossen und zugleich dekolletiert. Modell: E. Ungaro. Ohrringe: M. Moritz.

<u>Rechts:</u> Die Versuchung. Geschlitztes Etuikleid aus dunkelgrünem Samt. Halsausschnitt, Schulter und Ärmel mit kostbaren Pailletten bestickt. Modell: Yves Saint Laurent. Accessoires: Yves Saint Laurent. Smoking: Pierre Cardin. Haare: Frédérique für Mod's Hair. Make-up: Linda Mason für Helena Rubinstein.

84

*Denis Piel fotografierte im Hotel „Le Bristol", Paris.*

Spreads from German Vogue November 1979 fashion story ph. Dennis Peal It all looked too serious so I added speech bubbles, which upset Dennis at the time. I had already cut his cover in half, just to show the girl's eyes.

<u>Links:</u> Für sie, die ihren Stil gefunden hat: Korsage und Jacke aus schwarzem Samt. Karotaftrock mit Volant in kräftigen, klaren Farben (Stoff: C. J. Bonet). Modell: M. Schneider. Schmuck: B. Lambert. Schuhe: Maud Frizon.

<u>Rechts:</u> Für sie, die lieber ein bißchen mehr anhat: Gelber Seidenoverall mit schwarzem Samtmantel, passend mit gelbem Seidenjaquard gefüttert und goldpaspeliert. Modell: Studio-Dress (Stoff: Overall von Schwarzenbach & Co. Mantel von Scheibler Pelzer) Schmuck: M. Moritz. Schuhe: Ch. Jourdan. Er trägt einen Smoking von Hugo Boss. Hemd von Kern, Fliege von Taro. Haare: Ludovic für J.-L. David. Make-up: Ramon für Revlon.

*Denis Piel*

88

Still-life promotion for German Vogue 1979 ph. Ed White

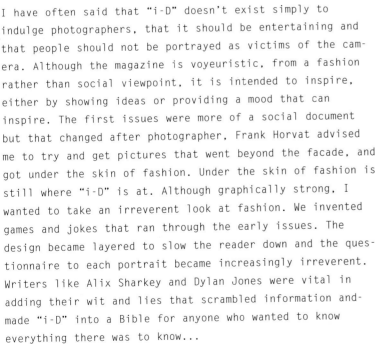

I have often said that "i-D" doesn't exist simply to indulge photographers, that it should be entertaining and that people should not be portrayed as victims of the camera. Although the magazine is voyeuristic, from a fashion rather than social viewpoint, it is intended to inspire, either by showing ideas or providing a mood that can inspire. The first issues were more of a social document but that changed after photographer, Frank Horvat advised me to try and get pictures that went beyond the facade, and got under the skin of fashion. Under the skin of fashion is still where "i-D" is at. Although graphically strong, I wanted to take an irreverent look at fashion. We invented games and jokes that ran through the early issues. The design became layered to slow the reader down and the questionnaire to each portrait became increasingly irreverent. Writers like Alix Sharkey and Dylan Jones were vital in adding their wit and lies that scrambled information and-made "i-D" into a Bible for anyone who wanted to know everything there was to know...

In autumn 1979 I was asked by German "Vogue" to help the art director Helmut Schmidt. I proposed a spread with the headline "Aaaaaa!". We photographed very expensive crystal glasses in a table setting. I used Ed White to make a 5x4 shoot of a cocktail being thrown into a glass. It took two days to get right; the colour of the drink, the exposure and my aim into the glass. No one else would throw the drink as each smashed throw had to be cleaned up.

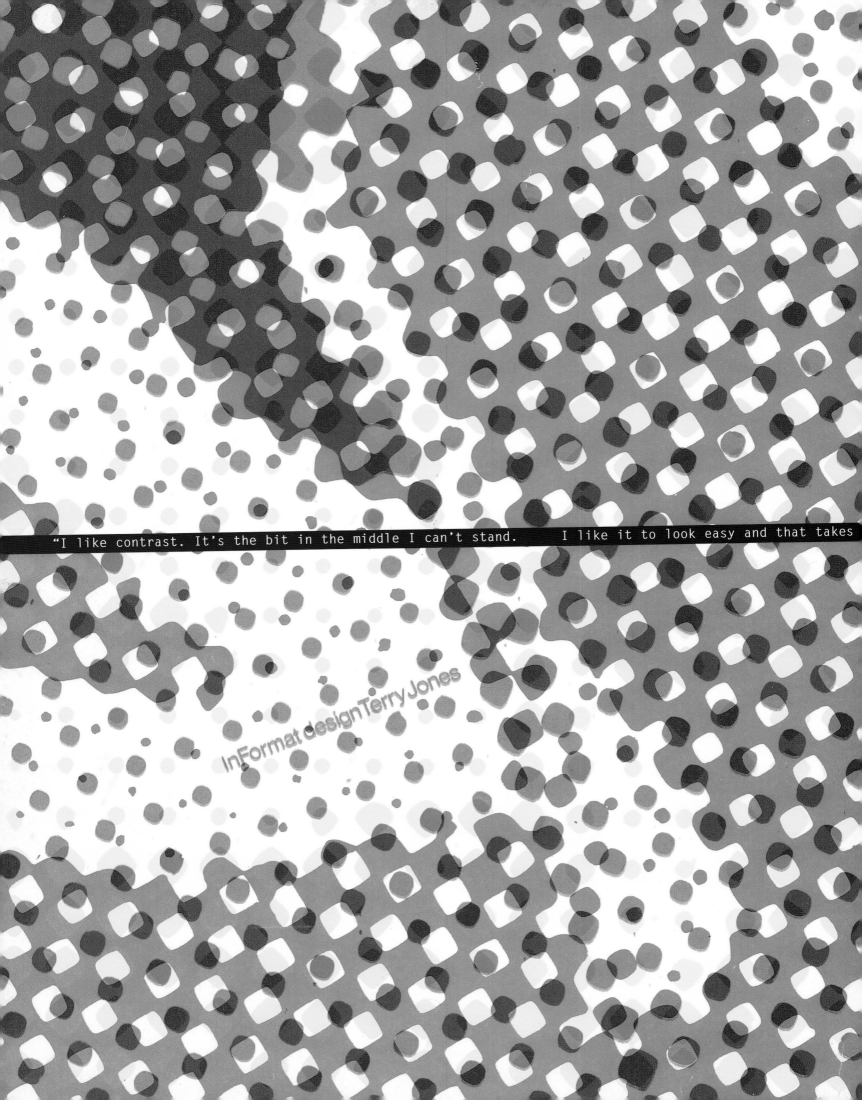

"I like contrast. It's the bit in the middle I can't stand.        I like it to look easy and that takes

InFormat designTerry Jones

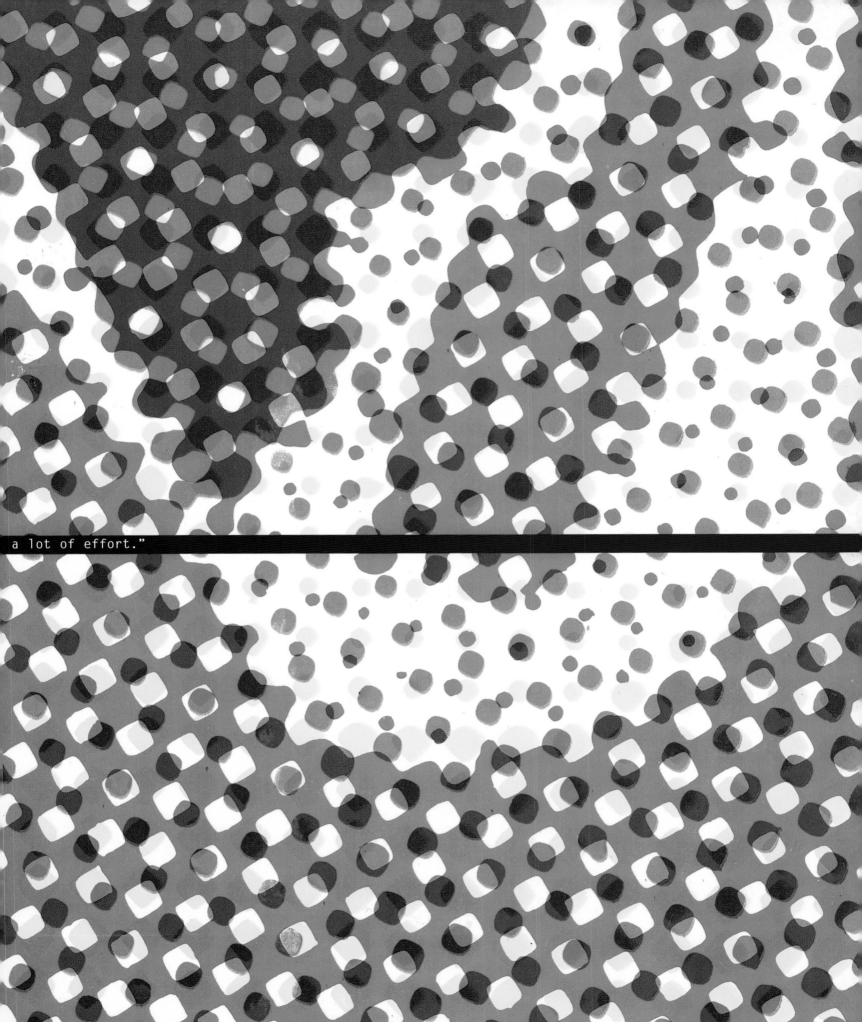

a lot of effort."

## POLAROID

POLAROID
Miracolo della tecnica. La foto istantanea
è uno strumento perfetto per l'Instant Design.
Consente di risparmiare tempo nella preparazione
dei bozzetti, può essere usata come esecutivo finale.
Ho cominciato a usare la Polaroid SX 70
quando ero Art Director a *British Vogue*,
per una copertina: un viso su un fondo rosso.
Sapevo che la saturazione del rosso era molto buona
su quella pellicola. Oliviero Toscani ci lavorò sopra,
realizzando solo 12 scatti.
Lo stampatore era stupito, ma i risultati furono ottimi.
Su *i-D*, usiamo la nuova *"Image System"* per registrare
le mode della strada.
In un certo senso si può dire che la Polaroid
ha influenzato il concetto stesso con cui è nata la
rivista e il tipo di impaginazione.

**instant DESIGN**

British Vogue March '75
photo Toscani   art TJ

it's all
British
50 pages of best buys
from top to toe

126

"I like contrast, it's the bit in the middle I can't stand.
I like the end product to look easy and that takes a lot of
effort."

Choices, whether unconscious or conscious, effect our
lives. Every choice, whether large or small, adds up to our
sensory perception of the world. Catching all the sensory
fragments is what makes life worth living, that accumula-
tion of touch, taste, smell, sound and, of course, visuals.
Graphic design is about arranging marks or images and the
effect of one in relation to another, through size, colour
and position. Being a graphic designer means it's second
nature to make decisions within a predetermined framework,
an imposed discipline. It would be hard to be an artist and
to create without imposing some kind of problem which needs
to be solved, even though the idea of solutions being flexible within different contexts is more attractive. My basic
graphics toolbox is made up of: hand-marks from handwriting
to complete blobby alphabets; stencils, used for logos and
display; typewriter lettering, for text and display; computers, used both for lettering and images, degraded and
coarsened by raster screen technology; montage, from basic
cut, tear and stick, as used in early issues of "i-D", to
electronic collage using Scitex imaging systems or video
Paintbox.
I don't like the concept of perfection because it implies
finality. Everyone is a designer in the literal sense of
the word - making decisions. We make choices in every

aspect of daily life, from going to work via the quickest
route to arranging things on a shelf. Many of my graphic
techniques are cheap, and were developed so as to get the
most out of what was available at "i-D" in its earliest
days. Others appear cheap, but a montage made for "Vanity
Fair" was one of the most expensive spreads the magazine
ever printed.
All graphic solutions are influenced by the mass of
ephemera in life and society. Images are constantly thrown
around the brain day and night, and the imagination must be
fed with stimulation from music, film, architecture and
discussion. While at art college I felt there was a limit
to the amount I could learn. I was a pain in the arse for
my tutors because I wouldn't make a finished rough for the
projects they set. Art colleges should be a place to experiment and make mistakes, because it's necessary to know the
limits before you can stretch them.
I use a pallete of types. Avant-garde typefaces are an
unnecessary indulgence because we've still got the classics
- round, square, condensed, mechanical - to play with. A
typeface is a functional thing. Some can be used decora-
tively, others make a "bad taste" contrast. With two or
three typefaces you can produce an unlimited number of combinations because every time you put a word down the shape
and sense of the word will create that difference. Colour
is another thing I use in contrast. Because most of the
work I did as a student had to be printed, but students
weren't allowed in the print department, I began silk-

FASHION MAGAZINE No 1 50p

# i-D

i-D

love
hate
push
y-ft
kiss
wipe
misc
find
pet-
bcup
dcup
-vpl
noft
s-ex
stop
home
h-rt

sexsense

128

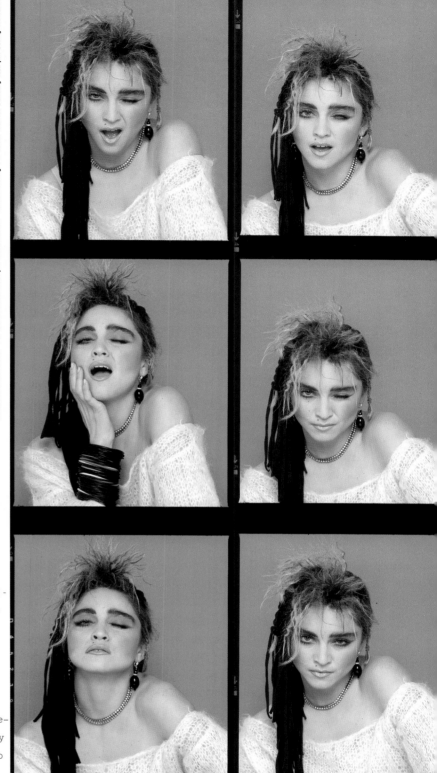

Madonna's first cover i-D No. 15 March 1984 ph. Mark Lebon   Neneh Cherry i-D cover No. 100 January 1992 ph. Jenny Howarth

screen printing, which is the basis of how I use colour. In the early days of "i-D" we went through the stage of functional legibility until we perfected the art of illegibility, when even the headlines needed subtitles! The layout was layered to slow the reader down.

Colin Fitzgerald, Latent Image colour house: "Terry has presented us with all sorts of things which he called art work, from balls of coloured string to bits of cardboard with threads stuck to it. One piece had 27 overlays with different breakdowns of colours on each. Everything he presents us with for repro has its own problems because Terry pushes the limits. One time we'd mistakenly transposed two colours in the proofing process, producing green flesh. I said we'd change it in the printing, but Terry said, don't worry, I like it. Another time he wanted to include all the colour bars and cut marks on the printed page, so I said, well can we take off our credit because someone might think the colour house have done a dreadful job!"

After producing every variation of layout over the years I now concentrate on using the best possible images. Today the design of "i-D" is minimal. After years of wearing street-style, fans of fashion began to crave traditional glamour. "i-D" anticipated the change, moving on from the grungy mashed-up look to simple minimalism and then to a modern, classic design. I go back to the same types and structures and find that they provide design solutions which remain contemporary. After being invited by Linotype Hell to attend the Typo Media conference in Frankfurt I was convinced to change type, from Futura to Avenir and Lubalin Graph to Cecilia, thanks to meeting the type design Maestro Adrian Frutiger.

He is a man in 82 who has kept up with what is new.The new cuts of Univers have been added to the digital range, which we are now using in i-D. The Types I use on the covers of the magazine reflect the changes we are making inside and add graphics news to the fashion.

No 100 JANUARY 1992 £1.80

# i-D

**i-D MAGAZINE**
-DEAS, FASHION, CLUBS, MUSIC, PEOPLE

neneh cherry
strictly personal

# think
# positive!
## be aware if you dare

## 100th issue special

action on AIDS:
positive responses from fashion, music, film,
photography, sport and activism.

pull-out club supplement:
new directions in clubland

free condom inside!

USA $5.50

01

9 770262 357006

FRANCS 33 LIRE 6,500 DM 12,50 PESETAS 665 D KR 49

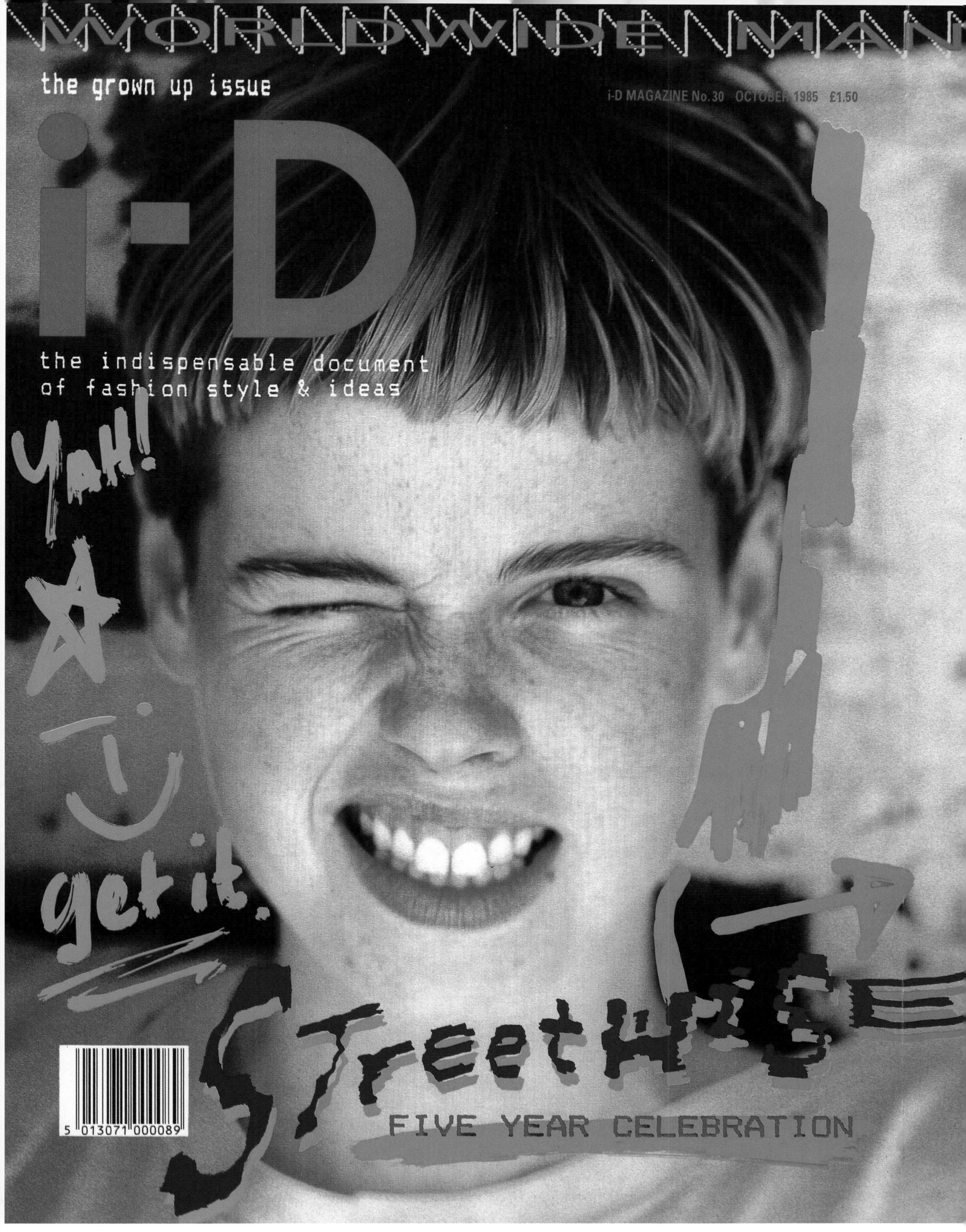

WORLDWIDEMAN

the grown up issue

i-D MAGAZINE No.30   OCTOBER 1985   £1.50

# i-D

the indispensable document
of fashion style & ideas

YAH!

get it.

Streetwise

FIVE YEAR CELEBRATION

5 013071 000089

i-D cover No. 30 October 1985

# EVerthing
## BEFORE IT

WHAT DOES APATHY MEAN?

I CAN'T
BE BO
TO FIN
OUT

Wide-rib zip cardi coat by Richmond/
Cornejo for Joseph, approx. £45; Black &
White leggins by The Cloth, £28.95 at
Jones, Liberty, The Warehouse Glasgow
and Koko Dublin; Cap £9.50 from Big Apple
Hyper Hyper.

38

S DIFFERENT

CHANGED

ERED

E RED

LIFE
IS LIKE
AN ASHTRA

FULL OF
LITTLE
DOUBTS

Barbara De Vries face hood poloneck &
leggins, £32 at Harvey Nichols; 2nd hand
man's jacket worn as skirt from a selection
at Blaks, Sicilian Ave WC2, from £15; Doc
Marten lace-ups £28.99 at Office Shoes Hyper Hyper.

Spread from i-D Green issue 1986 ph. Marc Lebon, the moderl is Jenny Howarth

起きて着たい服を着る。これが僕だ。それだけのことだ。

音楽で世界は変わる

# LENNY KRAVITZ
of the world

レニー・クラヴィッツ インタビュー

インタビュー・文=高橋 健太郎
写真=荒木 経惟

とうとうヤツがやって来た。90's にたったひとり、世界を相手に正面切って愛を歌う男、レニー・クラヴィッツ。i-D JAPAN は殺人的なスケジュールで世界を飛び廻るヤツ、レニー・クラヴィッツを電光石火のダイビングキャッチ。おまけに天才アラーキーが、ヤツの最高イカしたショットを"爆写"してくれた。神童と天才がスパークし合う、まさに歴史的なセッション。このゴーカ企画は A 級保存印！

23 i-D JAPAN

i-D JAPAN

いったい「普通」って何なんだよ。

差別はシステムを維持するためにある。

俺たちが政治的だとしたら、それは俺たちが生きてきた状況そのものが、どうしようもなく政治的なものだったからだよ。

i-D JAPAN 29

今日、自分がこの世に存在してから十五年がたち、そして、十年代後半にも入ろうとしている。この十五年の間にさまざまなことに出会ってきたと自分は感じます。（中略）自分は小学校一年から三年生にかけて充分さまざまなことを学んだり、転車に乗っていた頃近くにあった岩に友達と話そうと思い後を向いたりと覚えています。（中略）いろいろな所に顔やいろいろな頭の中にぶつきりと覚えています。（中略）自分という頭の中にぶつき病院へ行くということもつっこんでいき岩のかどにぶつかり怪我をしました。それは自た。しかし今ははっきりいうとこのような怪我をしていてよかったという面も感じています。それは怪我ということに、気をつけよう又注意しようというような事が自然に身についたと自分は思います。

自分を知る
四十六番 花田光司

取材·文=小池 光雄
取材協力=土屋 明子
写真提供=©Sports Graphic NUMBER

中学校一年、本名簿時の貴花田光司くん。パチ太郎と呼ばれたい！

スーパースターはやっぱりスキャンダラスだった。「無口な青年」などとは、誰が言ったか真赤なウソ。真実は、藤島部屋のおひざもと、中野区中野本町にあり。揺れば出てくる超わんぱくエピソードの数々。カラオケ・ナイト・クルージング……。ワイルドな小学校時代、門限破りのカラオケ・ナイト・クルージング……。ラブリーな素顔。ああ、やっぱり、こんな貴花田が好きッ！

**ついに貴花田、スキャンダル発覚!?**

---

### キョンキョン・ドキドキインタビュー

マイッタ、マイッタ。そわそわして、注射打つ順番待ってるガキみたいな心持ち。なんでったってキョンキョンだもの。ドキドキ、タバコ喫う。ムセる。"グッド・イナフ"のTシャツ着たキョンキョン、イキナリのヤボな質問？ ハジマッチャック!!

i-D（以下i）目覚まし時計は何個使ってるの？
小泉（以下k）使いません。起きちゃうんだもん。チャンと、夜ふかしはねゼンゼンするんだけど、なんか4時とか5時に寝ても9時とかに自が勝ちうその。ババァみたいでしょ。
i 「ひみつのアッコちゃん」と「キューティーハニー」ならどっちになってみたい？
k ハニー！
i もしも、自分がオランダに生まれたとしてチューリップと風車だったらどっちになってみたい？
k チューリップ。基本的に花、好きなんですよ。チューリップとか好きですよー。
i それじゃ、ひまわりとチューリップだったら？
k チューリップ！ ひまわりはも悲しくってダメです。
i 太陽に向いてるっていうイメージがあるから？
k なんか悲しい、チューリップのがいいな!!
i 朝顔とチューリップだったら？
k 朝顔もあんまり……朝顔より、チューリップ!!
i キョンキョンとキスしたらどんな顔するのかな？
k さぁー。子供の頃もそんなに思わないで過ごしてたし、あたし、とってもそういうことに対して、疎かったですよ。
i ウブだった？
k うん。みんなが言ってるとか、意味わかんなかった。話してるのダマッて聞いてた。
i ショージキさと、ちょっぴりウソつきとどっちが好きですか？
k あたし、ショージキって見たことないからよくわからない（一同笑う）
i もうヤダラアタマきてる。「こんど許さん」って入ってます？
k あたし、あんまり嫌いなヒトにっていいってないですね。ハゲくんムついたりしない、ムカついたらそこで言ってしまう。そのままにしたり、あやるような子でないって耐えられない。
i じゃあ、おっきいパンツと小さいパンツとどっちが好き？
k あたしおっきいパンツの方が好きです／
i それじゃあ、"大きいLOVE"と"小さいLOVE"では？
k 与えるのは"大きいLOVE"、仕事なんかって的なLOVE。でも、"小さいLOVE"もなきゃヤだな、ラブリーな感じのLOVE。
i 2年目だったキョンキョンの「ライ麦畑でつかまえて」発見であるあきもドカッと売れたっていうのがわかるよね。
k あれね、あたし読んでなかったのね（笑）。読んでなかった。後から一同大笑い。何かの番組で「今読んでる本は何ですか」って聞かれて、とっさにその日に「ライ麦畑」、1ページぐらいは読んでたから「今日はコレ待ってます」み、1ページはじめのとこだけ読んでてずっとそのまま棚にあるでしょ？ そしたらあんなふうな人になっちゃったから。
i 読んでみたらどうだった？
k ウン。面白かったけど、そんなにスゴくってのはなかった。でもボクもハズカシながら読んだのは4年ぐらい前で、吉本興業言ったら、500円のビンもも飛んだりして（笑）、ショージキ言って本当に好きじゃなかったりして、あやるようなよ。
k そう、ですよね。もっとはやく読んだらね。せめて10代の時にね。読む本だと。
i じゃ、いま"若モン"としてのスバラシって感じる？
k 若いからね、感じることもいいって言う"若いって"のは、考えなくていいことだと思う。それは──、なんか、なんか、若いんだもん。
i それじゃあ、逆にいま"オトナ"になった気分はどう？
k "オトナ"とかっていうのはないね。オトナでもコドモもいっしょっていうか？"イイゴ"は"イイゴ"だし"ヨクナイゴ"は悪いし。オトナとカドモとか繊細とかじゃないね。キビシクなりました。自分より若いからって許せないこともイッパイあるし。
i キビシクなったのは？
k こういう仕事始めてからとか思います。ちっちゃい子供とかにね、自分がいたいところにある物を取れてっていうのは間違ってると思うけど、そこにあるものを取ってあげる必要が

いってっていう感じが大人になったらスゴクある。子供に対しても上の人に対しても。
i 世の中にあふれてる自分のパブリック・イメージには、イッペン満足してますか？
k なんか満足っていうか、ジメジメとかって思う。撮影のときやコマーシャルとか、仕事だから真剣にやってますよ。
i 出回ったものについては「なんか違う」って不満は？
k あり得ない、です。
i キョンキョンがこなしてるキャラクターなりタレントっていう存在は、他の誰かと替え効くと思う？
k それはもう、私はコレはホントの仕事だからね。名前も、顔も、声も、体も、全部が売迄商品のハズでしょ？ 私しなくても、この仕事してるは誰も替わりはいない。一世一代限りの仕事だから。うん。
i キョンキョンって、それこそメディアの波に流されて、自由自在になってが！ 波乗りしてるように思うんですが？ 自分のなかで、いろいろゴッチャになってるかとか？ "ザ・オリジナル・キョンキョン" かわからなくなっちゃう時は？
k ない、まったく。みんなワタシですよ。
i みんなワタシ。
k ウン
i ウン。
**ホントの自分なんてないよね、つんなんじゃないよねって！！** 
もし恋愛して恋人がいたらちゃんとフィフティー・フィフティーでいたいし、オンナっていうより私は私、でいたい」で、それならいう時でも、その瞬間の自分なんで。だから過去にも未来にもつなげな
**ホントの自分なんて最初っからどこにも無くて、あると思わない。全部自分。ホントも何もないよ。** すっごくやさしい時があった。すっごくワルい時があっても気にしない"ホントのあたしはやさしい"とかってなんかいそんな一瞬の自分だって。だから過去にも未来にもつなげないまごいういう自分で。
i 「愛しても」って相手の目を見開えて言うコトは難しい？
k そんなの、愛したら言えますよ。セイセイ堂々、抱き締めて言えます。ウン。
i "ラブ・アンド・ピース"ってコトバは？
k なんかね、あたりまえのことね。みんなラブ・アンド・ピースってなわけ言わなきゃいけないのはミョー気もするけど、私まの仕事ってそういうコトづ伝えていけるし、政治家より早いなと思う。ちょうとすってね、ちょっでそうもんなんだけれども。でも、自分が早いなかでもんなことさ言おうとしてできっこない。自分自身がホントに楽しんで、仕事も生活も友とも、仕事とかホントに楽しくてたまらないまで。

"普段着でも普段は何でもいいの、モンペでもなんでも。歩きやすかったりするのが朝そこにあるものを着るカンジ""仕事ってなんか育てて、それで評価がチがってしまうんじゃツマンナイ"って言ってるキョンキョン。なんだ、キョンキョン、ココにいるじゃん。明日からキャラパティがパカと何かして知ったこっちゃないけど、とにかくどのキョンキョンも全部キョンキョン!! ✪

（インタビュー・文=i-D編集部 村松哲哉）

写真=ホンマ タカシ
29歳 乙女座 血液型不明 東京都出身
スタイリング=池田 美智子
年齢不詳 射手座 AB型 東京都出身
ヘア・メーク=山崎 彰
29歳 水瓶座 B型 神奈川県出身

ラブ・アンド・ピースってあたりまえなのにね。

ホント

ほ、ネ、読んでなかったの『ライ麦畑』
小泉 今日子 KYONO

# CLEAN

シュガー吉永　24歳　ハハナエキンチカ（ギター）／この
ロードレーサーはお年から乗っている。都内の移動は自
転車が一番。でも、車の排気ガスには閉口する。春と秋
の風は気持ちいいけど。／防塵マスク（クリーンスクリー
ン in London）、カットソー¥11,000（シーズンパーツ
by　シート・シブヤ西式シート）、ベルト¥2,000（マリー
クヮント）、ストレッチパンツ　参考商品（ヴェールタンス）

JP 本能

マーヴィン／24歳／ムスタング系アスリート（ボール）／高校のときにストーンズのライブをビデオで見てショックを受け、サッカーから音楽に転向。ひとりでハーレムを歩いたとき、"動物状態"、つまり本能的な危険を感じた。ごく怖かった。

金 哉穂=インタビュー
危ないコトだらけの自分の人生が
一番デンジャラス。
ハービー 山口=写真

別府義明　手島いさむ　阿村一史　西川幸一

# ユニコーン
# 殺人未遂事件

# 完全犯罪

"ひき逃げ"によるユニコーン殺人未遂事件は、とんでもないどんでん返しで意外な結末を見ることになった。

大作『服部』、昨年の正三段スライドアルバムリリース。そして「ヒゲとボイン」へと連鎖するたくみなプロット。ステージでの大バカぶりをおくびにも出さないポーカーフェイス。まったくもって、なんて危険な完全犯罪、なんてそう。殺されかけたのはユニコーンではなく、我々だ。じわじわと、原因はただひとつ。じわじわと、音もなく身体を蝕む"ユニコーン中毒"によって——

43  i-D JAPAN

人とクルマと自然が共に生きること。
私たち、日産グループは、「共生」をポリシーとして、
2000年に向かっています。

we
are
what
we
br(eat)h

Tillandsia meduseae　チランドシア・メデューサ
**Air Plant**と呼ばれるアナナス科の着生植物。
根は付着する機能しか持たず、葉から大気中の
水分を取り込むことで生きている。

日産グループ

Feel the Beat

WILLY BOGNER PRESENTS THE FIRE AND ICE TRIBE IN SEARCH OF CHIT'NA

TEN ESSENTIALS TO TAKE INTO THE WILDERNESS OF ALASKA: 1. A SENSE OF HUMOR 2. A SLEEPING PARTNER TO CURE HYPO–THERMIA 3. YOUR OWN MOOSEHEAD BEER, BECAUSE BUYING A ROUND WILL BUST YOUR BUDGET 4. A LAUGHING MACHINE TO AVOID CLOSE ENCOUNTERS WITH FURRY FRIENDS 5. STRONG REPELLENT TO AVOID BEING EATEN ALIVE BY "NOSEEUMS" AND OTHER UNIDENTIFIED FLYING OBJECTS 6. LAYERS OF FIRE AND ICE CLOTHING SO YOU CAN PEEL DOWN TO YOUR PERSONAL ESSEN-TIALS AS THE TEMPERATURE SHOOTS FROM -60° TO +32° 7. UM...

THIS FIRE AND ICE FALL/WINTER 93/94 CATALOG CONTAINS SIX PAGES DESCRIBING THE TRIBE'S SEARCH FOR CHIT'NA. IF YOU USE ALL YOUR SIX SENSES - YOU WILL FIND YOUR OWN WAY TO CHIT'NA. THE FIRE AND ICE CATALOG WAS MADE POSSIBLE BY THE FOLLOWING PEOPLE: THE AGENCY .START ADVERTISING, THE DIRECTOR TERRY JONES, THE PHOTOGRAPHERS STEFAN RUIZ, THOMAS KALAK AND VIANNEY TISSEAU, THE ART ASSISTANT PETRA LANGHAMMER, THE GUIDING OF DOUGH COOMBS, THE COOKING OF KEVIN, THE LODGING OF MIKE AND TSAINA LODGE, THE FLYING OF CHET SIMMONS, THE SNOWBOARDS OF RAD AIR, THE GLASSES OF OAKLEY AND B+W SPORTTRADE, THE BOOTS OF NORTHWAVE, THE HELPING HANDS OF TRICIA AND REINHARD, THE TIPS OF JOHN EAVES, THE TRUST OF WILLY BOGNER AND ALL THE PEOPLE AT FIRE & ICE. THE TRIBE: BARBARA, ANGI, MARION, ULI, RETO, KIWI, JOST AND TYRON

where the hell is Chit'na?

i-D 1983 ph. Nick Knight, Thomas Degen

VIBES...
A MIRROR...
A FILTER...
A FEW FRAGMENTS...
THE OCCASIONAL
RED HERRING...
SOME DUFF GEN...
AND A FEW CLUES
TO WAKE YOU UP
TO WAR AND
HEALTH...
THE GAME
STARTS HERE...
ARE YOU
PLAYING...

142

Photo Nick Knight

4    "I design for people who have forgotten their clothes and are getting

# vibes

# THE FUTURE IS OUR RESPONSIBILITY

Sherron Waugh, singer with Savajazz, wearing 'WORLDWIDE NUCLEAR BAN NOW' silk T-SHirt from the "Choose Life" series by Katherine Hamnett. The collection includes 'Education Not Missiles', 'Ban Pollution', 'Save The World'. Profits to go to a child care charity.

Katherine believes that everyone should take a responsibility for life. You have to find ways of making your viewpionts noticed - so after having her designs copied worldwide, the originator of the crushed silk look and pre-washed cotton has produced a propaganda series; she wants to be 'ripped off' worldwide. So get to it mein chers amigos!

Sherron says: "I don't have political allegiances though I support CND because no-one else seems to care. Basically we all have the right to live, I don't want my child to grow up in a world of no future, no hope."

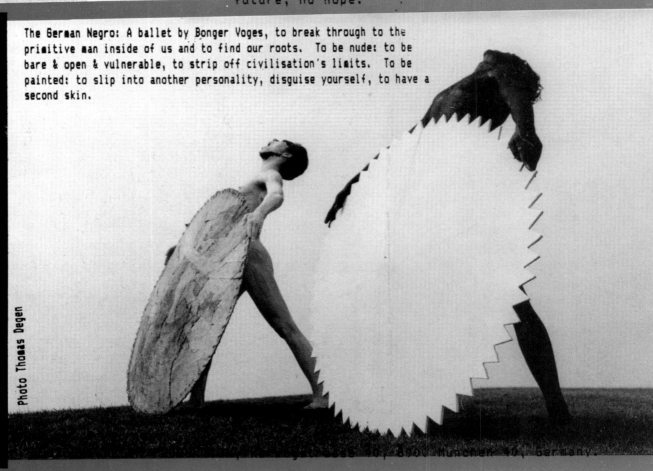

The German Negro: A ballet by Bonger Voges, to break through to the primitive man inside of us and to find our roots. To be nude: to be bare & open & vulnerable, to strip off civilisation's limits. To be painted: to slip into another personality, disguise yourself, to have a second skin.

Photo Thomas Degen

Mental energy and clear objectives have more positive power than unfocused aggressive frustration. Media Manipulation influences more political decisions than ever. Interact with your media environment.

**LEARN from the Past**
**LIVE for the Present**
**SPARE A THOUGHT for the Future**

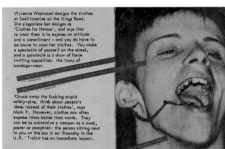

Vivienne Westwood designs the clothes
at Seditionaries on the Kings Road.
She sloganises her designs as
'Clothes for Heroes', and says that
to wear them is to express an attitude
and a commitment – and you do have to
be brave to wear her clothes. You make
a spectacle of yourself on the street,
and a spectacle is a show of force
inviting opposition: the irony of
bondage-wear.

'Chuck away the fucking stupid
safety-pins; think about people's
ideas instead of their clothes', says
Mark P. However, clothes can often
express ideas better than words. They
can be as subversive a weapon as a book,
poster or pamphlet; the person sitting next
to you on the bus in an 'Anarchy in the
U.K.' T-shirt has an immediate impact.

**Photographs of King's Road punks taken in summer 1976 by
Steve Johnston. Pages from "Not Another Punk Book"
published in 1978, by Aurum Press.**

Spread from "Not Another Punk Book"

146

"YOU HAVE TO DESTROY TO CREATE" MALCOLM McLAREN

THE ABILITY TO LAUGH AT THE THING

SITUATION 3

VIVIENNE WESTWOOD PHOTOGRAPH BY NORMA MORICEAU

WHILE STILL TAKING IT SERIOUSLY HAS VIRTUALLY DISAPPEARED

this disgraceful 'T'-shirt printed is punished firmly.

They must be Russians. — Irene Harri... North Chailey, Sussex.

IT IS ...

under...

civ...

with...

M. Burkes, Kent.

I PROTEST ... article and abo... picture in the

NOT ANOTHER PUNK! BOOK

AURUM PRESS

NOT ANOTHER PUNK BOOK

Shi...

THE outrageous Sex Pistols shoot back into Britain's homes tonight . . . on BBC TV.

The punk rockers will appear on Top of the Pops, the favourite show of millions of ¿teenyboppers

They will sing their new disc Pretty Vacant, in a filmed recording which is described by its director as "pretty eccentric."

The BBC decision to put the punk rockers on TV is certain to enrage thousands of parents and other viewers. For the group — who

BBC rais... on the S...

include Johnny Rot... and Sid Vicious — caused two furth... storms recently. STORM No 1 when the group a... on Thames TV programme and the air with f... words.

Banr...

STORM ... when they... leased an... record ... Queen.

BANG...

co.

ISBN 0 906053 06 4
£2.50 NET

NOT ANOTHER PUNK! BOOK

Cover of Punk Book published in 1978    single sleeve The Black Petty Booshwah designed by Zebulon 1979

Denis & M. mode:ex basement 5.
denis is wearing
suit from
Kenny's shop,was
about £25 three years
ago,white shirt
and bow
tie from
junk shop,shoes
about £60
from the natural
boot store in
neal street,glasses 25p.
likes:listening
to the radio
and tv together,
24hrs a day"I'm
like a walking camera
and tape recorder.
dislikes:nosey people.

M wearing dark
suit and shirt from junk
shop.boots from ravels,
glasses about
a quid.
he's a rhythm
machine,one of the best
drummers around.
denis and M,now of
Urban Shakedown,
have just been recording with
martin hanett.the
music is totally different
to basement 5,definately
dance music but
nothing likes whats
around now.the 2 of them
will be gigging
round about christmas
-travelling road show with a difference-
"bring your party
hat and your dancing shoes".

152

susana frye

Spread from i-D No.6   PIL logo

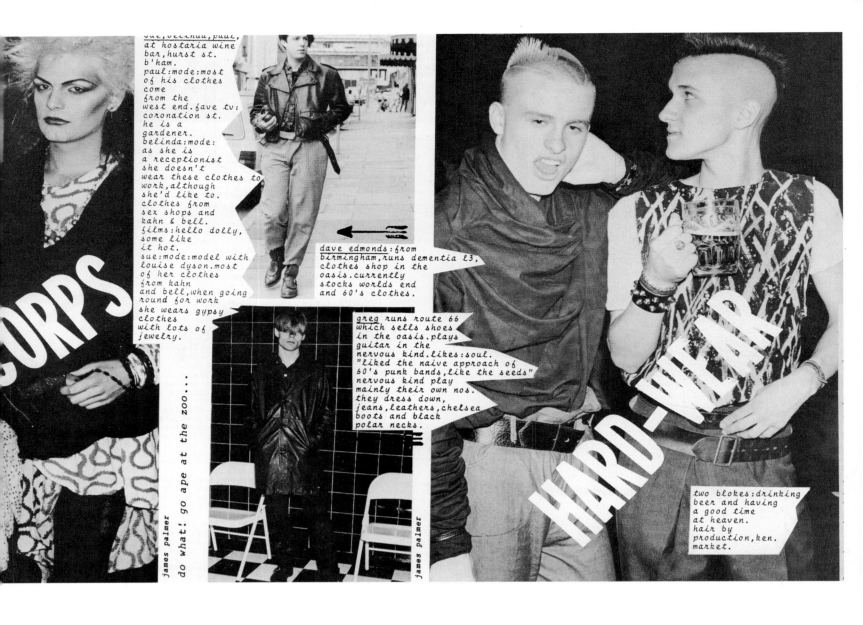

**CORPS**

sue,belinda,paul,
at hostaria wine
bar,hurst st.
b'ham.
paul:mode:most
of his clothes
come
from the
west end.fave tv:
coronation st.
he is a
gardener.
belinda:mode:
as she is
a receptionist
she doesn't
wear these clothes to
work,although
she'd like to.
clothes from
sex shops and
kahn & bell.
films:hello dolly,
some like
it hot.
sue:mode:model with
louise dyson.most
of her clothes
from kahn
and bell,when going
round for work
she wears gypsy
clothes
with lots of
jewelry.

james palmer

do what! go ape at the zoo...

dave edmonds:from
birmingham,runs dementia £3,
clothes shop in the
oasis.currently
stocks worlds end
and 60's clothes.

greg runs route 66
which sells shoes
in the oasis.plays
guitar in the
nervous kind.likes:soul.
"liked the naive approach of
60's punk bands,like the seeds"
nervous kind play
mainly their own nos.
they dress down,
jeans,leathers,chelsea
boots and black
polar necks.

james palmer

**HARD-WEAR**

two blokes:drinking
beer and having
a good time
at heaven.
hair by
production,ken.
market.

## FASHION TIP (B) STEVIE STEWERT
# "MO STOF THESPYS THATCOMET O OURSH OWS AR EN'TALL OWEDIN."

**STEVIE:** "I'm not into spying at all. I never used to spy when I was at college – and I don't now – so I don't see why other people should do it. If you go to see somebody's fashion show, it belongs to them – not you. Most of the spys that come to our shows aren't allowed in, but you can't do anything about the ones that do get through. We're not divulging anything about our show this year, we're keeping it very secret. We haven't chosen the music yet but we will be using accessories by Layla D'Angelo as well as our own. In Paris we showed a capsule menswear collection that we are trying out – we will show a token piece of it at our English show, and it will be available for viewing at Lynn Franks showroom. Our English show is going to be a lot more abstract than our previous shows – why? – because Bodymap love to change! I won't be going to anybody else's fashion shows this season – there *are* people I would like to poison during fashion week, but I'm not saying who!" STEVIE STEWERT and DAVID HOLAH'S BODYMAP show is in the Marjani tent on March 15th.

## FASHION TIP (D)
# "DE NIM!!?"

**STUART, JOHN & PETER** – Buyers at **JONES.**

1. *Whose shows will you be checking out this season?*
Paul Raymonds
2. *Which places are the best for buying abroad?*
Bangkok
3. *What tips have you for fashion spys?*
Denim!!?
4. *How are buyers treated at fashion shows?*
When you spend between:-
£5,000 – £10,000 A sandwich and cup of tea. £10,000 – £20,000 Cold platter and Champagne. £20,000 – £50,000 Salt beef on Rue St. Denis! (Paris).
5. *Are there any new designers that you will be stocking this autumn?*
Yes
6. *What will you be looking out for during fashion week?*
Openings!
7. *Do you regard yourselves as spys?*
But of course not, Comrade.
8. *Is there anyone you'd like to poison during fashion week?*
Last years salt beef?!!

| | WHICH FAMOUS CELEBRITY BROKE THEIR ... A BENEFIT FOR THE CITY ROADS DRUG CO ... CENTRE IN LONDON ON JAN 18th 1985? |
|---|---|
| A | LENNY HENRY |
| B | PAUL WELLER |
| C | CAPTAIN SENSIBLE |

154

| | ROSE BY ANY OTHER NAME WOULD SMELL AS SWEET"? |
|---|---|
| A | ROMEO, IN ROMEO AND JULIET BY SHAKESPEARE |
| B | JULIET, IN ROMEO AND JULIET BY SHAKESPEARE |
| C | MERCUTIO IN ROMEO AND JULIET BY SHAKESPEARE |

**ROSE'S** best memory: Tickling match with my brother, who recently sailboarded around the entire British coast. Fave book: 100 years of solitude (Marquez). Recurring dream: being chased by flapping swans. Fave people: Harold Macmillan/Weather Girls. Hated habits: people with smelly armpits. Fave club: M-Dive at Roxannes Harrington Gardens. Rose's biggest secret: Not telling, because I promised him I wouldn't.

MAGENTA CYAN

**AFTER** two years of the Hip Hop scene in Britain, there have been many changes, the latest being a tracksuit price war. How many people are prepared to spend one hundred pounds for a good name? i-D travelled to the depths of EASTON to put the legendary Phase 2 crew in the hotspot about their clothes, image and Ready Brek adverts.

How important was their image as a crew?

LEE: "Where a lot of people are confused, they see designer clothes as part of breakin'..."

ALVIN: "Adidas ain't rated here any more. You can get a good tracksuit for £40 although people who come back from places like Italy say it's rated there. £80 and over. A while back we bought any old Adidas top or jeans but that's how things are..."

LEE: "The latest craze is ski gear."
DEAN: "...from a shop in 'Beau Street'."
LEE: "Ski goggles that you can buy around £70 for a good set, in bright colours and ski jumpers but that's our own..."

Why are people willing to pay these prices at the moment?

SIMON: "Most people have got at least one designer thing now. It's a fashion of it's own I suppose but it's evolved from breakin'."
LEE: "Even Dean's got a pair of NIKE trainers (The junior Phase 2 whizz-kid). When I was his age, I had the little black ones with the lace ups."
Take PRINGLE for example. That's a very good make of designer clothes...

Barton Hill. A lot of the skinheads have turned 'casuals' or 'dressers'...

they're wearing TOSCINI and the good clothes now.
ALVIN: "Where the TOSCINI people can't dance or the white boys. If they've got a good tracksuit or jumper on, the pullin' up the sleeves, I'm not dancin', I'm gonna muck myself up in it, thats when it's just for dance.
LEE: "...like the READY BREK adverts. If you think of a break-dancer, you think of black grey, but...

...ose wears: Blue/grey nylon Nike jacket, approx £25; White tracksuit trousers with red/grey stripes. £10.99; White lace-up Nike shoes with blue trim £24.99. All from Olympus Oxford St d. White cotton chintz top £1 from secondhand shop. Jewellery from a selection by Adrien Mann.

...oto Nick Knight, assisted by Rob Gazelle, shot at Lipstick Studios; Styling Hellen Campbell; Make-up Tracie Martyn at Sessions; Hair Jackie Brooker at Trevor Sorbie; Model Rose Batstone.

...hy waste money buying the label, when you can save money by using your loaf? ...ress sense isn't sensible dressing or sense of dress – it's distorting the ...est & coming up with the best – get casual.

i-D March 1985 Spy issue ph. Nick Knight, we enlarged the Polaroid because we liked the quality as a background to type, this made it harder to read but succeeded in slowing down the reader

39

**TAIWAN POP STAR -**
WU SAN GIVES A CORUSCATING RENDITION OF 'THE GIRL FROM HIROSHIMA' AT A CHARITY SHOW - NOTE THE AGGRESSIVE POSTURE, THE MICROPHONE GRIP. DESPITE THE 'PRETTY LITTLE GIRL' DRESS AND RIBBON, SHE MEANS BUSINESS - BIG BUSINESS. SALES IN EXCESS OF 15 MILLION, OFFERS FROM HOLLYWOOD, ABSOLUTE ADORATION FROM HER FANS. MAKES MOST BRITISH POPSTARS LOOK OVERDRESSED AS WELL AS OVERWEIGHT.

Pink mini-dress £4.00 from Camden Market. Leather gloves £18.00 from John Lewis. USA watch £15.00 from American Classics, Kings Rd. Dr Marten shoes £16.95 (small sizes) from Holts, Kentish Town Rd.
Make-up by Kay Montana. Foundation & powder at Cosmetics A La Carte. Eye make-up by Barry M, no. 50, 41, 6, 43, 36. Lipstick from Charles Fox. Hair by Sandra at Premier.

**DELHI BELLY DANCER -**
KIDNAP VICTIM OF THE WHITE SLAVE TRADE AT THE AGE OF 15. LEARNED TO BELLY DANCE IN TURKEY BEFORE BEING SOLD TO THE GRAND MOGHUL AS A CONCUBINE. SHE HAS SINCE BECOME A FAVOURITE OF THE HAREM. SHE LOVES TO SMOKE HASHISH AND HAVE THE EUNUCHS RUB AROMATIC OILS INTO HER SHOULDERS, BACK AND THIGHS. HER SEXUAL PROWESS IS LEGENDARY. SHE HAS EXHAUSTED MANY LOVERS WITH TECHNIQUES DERIVED FROM KARMA SUTRA.

Dark indian colour taffeta - dyed silks from Borovicks, 16 Berwick St and other materials from Charing X Rd. Indian jewellery from any indin sari shop. Total less than £11. Make-up by Kay Montana. Model Sandra at Premier.
Foundation and powder at Cosmetics A L Carte. Black eye shadow, Shiseido. Eye liner & mascara, Mary Quant. Lipstick, Yves St Laurent. Drawing, wetted black eye shadow.

**MITZI GOES TO DEHLI...**
STYLING: MITZI LORENZ. PHOTOGRAPHS: ROGER CHARITY

32

33

Post sack smock dress and gauntlets by Christopher Nemeth available from Bazaar, 4 South Molton St, House of Beauty and Culture and Cuts, 41 Market St, Brighton. String and sack earrings by Judy Blame available from Bazaar and House of Beauty and Culture; Paper bags from Oxfam Shop. Thatched clogs from a Parisian Hardware Store.

Rope and Twig hat by Slag available from Kunst Boutique, 28 Wardour St. Soho W1. Smocked back coat and cotton ragged under skirt by John Galliano both available from Bazaar, 34 Brook St. and 4 South Moltdn St. W1 also Jones, 71 Kings Rd. SW3 and Midas, 22 Kings St. Manchester. Penny Bottle broach by Judy Blame from Bazaar W1. Extended sole shoe by John Moore available from Bazaar, Houe of Beauty and Culture, Jones WC2 and SW3.

44

45

top: Spread from i-D January 1984 No. 21 ph. Roger Charity   bottom: ph. Marc Lebon who worked with Roger in Bowstreet Studio

PHOTOGRAPHS AND THE ODD BIT OF STYLING: MARC LEBON STYLING: FRED POODLE AT HOME   HAIR, MAKE-UP AND BRILLIANT IDEAS : YVONNE GOLD FOR SCHUMI AT FORTNUM AND MASON   MODEL AND GOOD FUN: SARAH WINGATE AT Z AGENCY HELPING HANDS: EDDIE MONSOON

top: Spread from i-D 1986 ph. Marc Lebon   bottom: i-D May 1995 ph. Marc Lebon   Stylist Annette Aurell Annett Monheim

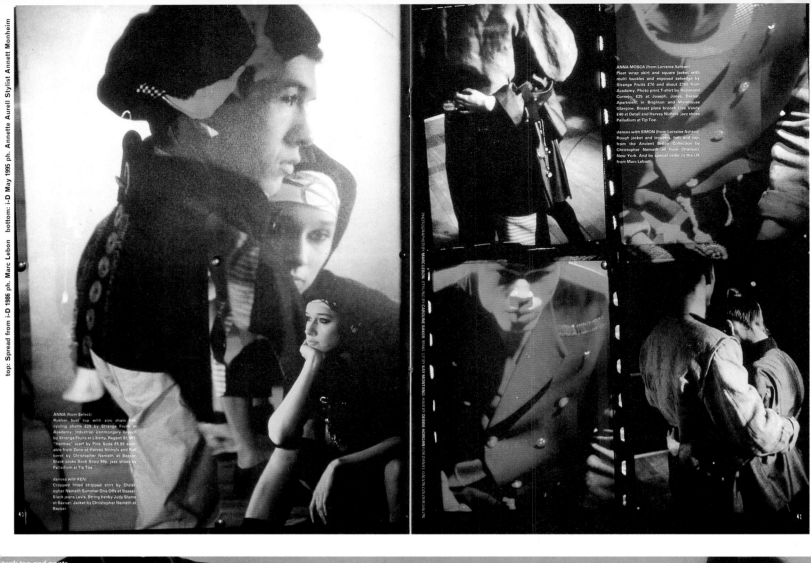

ANNA (from Select)
Rubber bust top with zinc chain and cycling shorts £29 by Strange Fruits at Academy. Industrial ironmongery brooch by Strange Fruits at Liberty, Regent St, W1. "Hermes" scarf by Pink Soda £5.99 available from Zone at Harvey Nichols and Puff beret by Christopher Nemeth at Bazaar. Black socks Sock Shop 99p, jazz shoes by Palladium at Tip Toe.

dances with KEN
Cropped fitted stripped shirt by Christopher Nemeth Summer One Offs at Bazaar. Black jeans Levis. String hanky Judy Blame at Bazaar. Jacket by Christopher Nemeth at Bazaar.

ANNA MOSCA (from Lorraine Ashton)
Pleat wrap skirt and square jacket with multi buckles and exposed selvedge by Strange Fruits £70 and about £185 from Academy. Photo print T-shirt by Richmond Cornejo, £25 at Joseph, Jones, Bazaar, Apartment in Brighton and Warehouse Glasgow. Breast plate brooch Lisa Vandy £40 at Detail and Harvey Nichols. Jazz shoes Palladium at Tip Toe.

dances with SIMON (from Lorraine Ashton)
Rough jacket and trousers, belt and cap, from the Ancient Briton Collection by Christopher Nemeth all from Charivari, New York. And by special order in the UK from Marc Lebon.

PHOTOGRAPHY BY MARC LEBON. STYLING BY CAROLINE BAKER. MAKE UP BY KAY MONTANO. HAIR BY DEBBIE MORGAN FOR DANIEL GALVIN. DANCERS ANNA AND SIMON

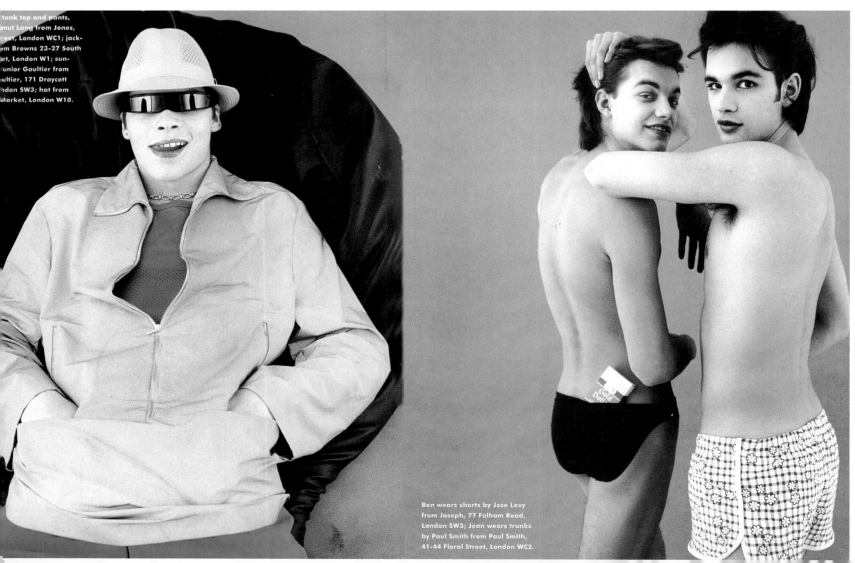

tank top and pants,
...mut Lang from Jones,
...reet, London WC1; jack-
...m Browns 23-27 South
...et, London W1; sun-
...unior Gaultier from
...ultier, 171 Draycott
...don SW3; hat from
...Market, London W10.

Ben wears shorts by Jose Levy from Joseph, 77 Fulham Road, London SW3; Jean wears trunks by Paul Smith from Paul Smith, 41-44 Floral Street, London WC2.

158

## DISCOTEQUE DARLINGS

Simon is dressed to go out to play .... HOT LAVA. People admired include Marlene Dietrich, Frank Finlay and Basil Brush. He is more than likely in the wrong place .... get back to those 1930s – decked out in Antony Price togs, ½ price sales tags, and red tag levis. Chocolate fudge slices from Europa stores are apparently the bees knees .... or the King's biscuit, preferably eaten by Noddy or Simon Bates. Best game: skipping. Best joke: 6" heels. High flung ladders .... stairways to heaven.

SIMON HOBART, who runs the KitCat club at Foxberts on Wed. evenings, wears Kahniverous cock-feather top, approx. £170; Kahniverous armwarmers £8; Kahniverous cheeky trousers, £28; Crotch piece £25 at Frisco Leathers; 8-inch boots £90 from Cover Girl on Upper St; Diamante earrings £13 at Kahniverous; Wigs from a selection at Kahniverous, £47; Funfur bracelets £5.50 at Kahniverous; Brass bracelets £5 each in Camden; Studded wrist band £15 at Frisco Leathers, silver bracelet £4 in Great Gear Market; Fake eyelashes and make-up by Charles Fox; Hair by Sparks in Great Gear Market, spruced up with Boots Firm Hold and Black & White, grease.

## FRISKY FOXY

"I would like to be the richest, nicest person in the entire world .... or a nun." Jane's favourite game is life .... or Hollywood – Yahoo!! She swoons to Tik & Tok and the HIPPOdrome .... swoons to The Kit Kat Club and the HIPPOdrome .... curves Montana (as in Claude), goes to The Kit Kat Club and wants to be healthy. When she was

JANE KAHN, designer, wears Kahniverous feather headress, approx. £190; Kahniverous sequined conical bra, approx. £60; Kahniverous diamante mittens, approx. £13; Old Terry De Haviland shoes; Earrings from Quasimodo Kings Rd, £29 each, necklaces from Quasimodo; Bracelets Butler & Wilson, approx. £34; Nose ring £3 at Birmingham ring market, nose pierced for £5 at Greater Gear Market – use ordinary stem earrings, bend the stem and do not put a stopper. Don't forget to take it out before you sneeze! Paste

CHEMICAL WARFARE WARRIOR

Judy would like to re-surface in ancient times, go diving, be baggy, and invite Scarlett round for supper. His favourite designers are Yohji Yamamoto, Rachel Auburn and Leigh Bowery. Club: Dive Bar. Record: Gladys Knight & The Pips – 'It Should've Been Me'. Popstar: Jimmy Healy. Judy has 10 basic outfits and 500 accesories ... has been a waitress in a dustbin and eaten synthetic cakes in packets. Judy knows that playing games is more important than winning, and that games are fun – fun – fun!!!

JUDY BLAME, jewellery designer, customised an old Burnstock & Spiers hat; Rubber top, £18 from Fetish Or Die; Rubber fisherman's wader £1,000 by Abel Villarreal – for more info write to 6412 Hollywood Blvd, Hollywood, C.A 90028; D.J rubber necklace to order from Judy Blame, and bracelets are a selection from his Chemical Warfare collection (spring/summer '85), ranging from £4 to £150. Info and orders on (01) 739 3988. Tattoo by Dave Baby, nipples pierced by Mr Sebastian, £28.

Judy Blame i-D August 1984 ph. Monica Curtain

NO.80

# i·D

## i·D MAGAZINE
### i-DEAS, FASHION, CLUBS, MUSIC, PEOPLE

©

THE DANGEROUS ISSUE

Legal raves + That Petrol Emotion + Fax fashion from the USA + Rebel MC

# Warning!
## This magazine is dangerous

## fashion fallout
### – poisonous looks

Water — is it safe to drink? ● Julian Clary, the man behind the make-up ● 'The Krays' and the Kemps — can pop stars act? ● Monie Love and the changing face of rap ● Viking Combat — have martial arts gone mad? ● Hip hop fashion adopts the suit ● The man behind 'The Toxic Avenger' ●

USA $4.95

05

9 770262 357006

FRANCS 33 LIRE 7.000 DM 12 PESETAS 665 D KR 49

bbeauty without cruelty
*Zoe* with white eye by Topolino.

TRAVEL: EARTH

STORY BY JEAN BAPTISTE MONDINO and JUDY BLAME
MAKE UP BY TOPOLINO
HAIR BY BARNABE
FASHION BY ZOE BEDEAUX (LONDON) and GIGI LE PAGE (PARIS)
CO ORDINATION BY YANNICK MORISOT
MODELS GURMIT, ROY BROWN AT UNIQUE, OLOK ZOE ANTHEA
BRYAN and JUDY BLAME

TEXT FROM EARTHDREAM BY ROBERT HAMILTON COURTESY OF GREEN BOOKS
ADDITIONAL INFORMATION: THANKS TO WAR ON WANT, CHRISTIAN AID, VOGUE

SPECIAL THANKS TO *TEMPO* MAGAZINE

# filthy rich dirty money

There are far too many tourists on spaceship Earth, and not nearly enough travellers. There are just too few people who feel that they really belong on this sacred little planet of ours. And that, quite simply, is why our future is threatened. Instead of taking joy from being in the world, and therefore wanting to experience and take care of it, the majority of people in the West, particularly those people of power and privilege, expend all their energy on having the things of the world, and consequently tour through life, uninvolved, irresponsible, unaware, intent just on collecting souvenirs. Unfortunately, there is a limit to how many such fare-dodging passengers the Earth can carry. *Robert Hamilton*

cut the crap
*Gurmit* wears net coat by Lionel Cros available from Lionel Cros shop (Paris) 4508 83411, scissor and cork chain by Judy Blame available to order on fax no. 071 289 4407 and nails model's own.

...OTOGRAPHY BY
...ONALD CHRISTIE
...YLING BY
...DY BLAME
...IR BY
...IL MOODIE
...R ZOO USING AVEDA
...KE-UP BY
...BBIE STONE
...PREMIER
...ODELS: MARTA
...STORM
...D GUY AT TAKE 2

# SCARED STIFF
sewing seeds on the crow road

Knit and silk scarf dress by Darryl Black from Regular Store, 16 Earlham Street, London WC2.

Coat and suit by Paul Smith from 40-44 Floral Street, London WC2 and Strand, 22 Queen Victoria Street, Leeds; fluorescent jacket by PS Paul Smith from Harvey Nichols, Knightsbridge, London SW5 and Van Mildert, 21 Elvert Bridge, Durham.

In Vietnam, epidemics of typhoid and hepatitis along the coast are the result of eating sewage-infected shellfish.

In 1984 a chemical company discharged detergent, bleach and caustic soda into the River Loddon destroying all life in the water.

In 1986, the dumping of sewage into the Thames had reduced the oxygen level so much that the Water Authority had to pump oxygen into the water to prevent large-scale deaths of fish.

Black bra from Portobello Market, skirt by Hamnett Active available from Fusion and feathers from Clignancourt Flea Market (Paris)

Spread from i-D December 1990 Dangerous issue ph. Jean-Baptiste Mondino Stylist Judy Blame

ESPRIT
COLLECTION

ESPRIT JEANS
SAN FRANCISCO, CALIF. 94107 - U.S.A.

ESPRIT
S P O R T

# WEAR CARE

"To shock is too easy. I don't want people to look like victims, patronised by the photographic process. I want to promote positive attitudes to life which aren't centred around consumerism or monetary status"

"Masters of Erotic Photography" showcased the work of twelve male photographers. I convinced the publishers Arum Press to do a book of "Women on Women" using such photographers as Debra Turberville, Sarah Moon and Alice Springs. It was 1977, when I was checking the proofs for the book in Verona, Italy and everyone kept asking me, so, what the fuck's punk? When I got back to London I started putting together "Not Another Punk Book".
In 1976 I set out to document punk fashion down the King's Road. I wanted to run the story in "Vogue" and asked Steve Johnson, a young photography student from Carlisle to make head to toe portraits against a white background. He found a piece of wall which served as his studio background and for three months stopped people at that spot. These pictures formed the basis for "Not Another Punk Book", published in 1978, while also setting a style of portraiture known as the straight-up, which we used at "i-D".
I went to San Francisco in the summer of 1989, and Doug Tompkins owner of Esprit who I'd met a few years back, invited us to stay as his guests. I'd been talking to John Godfrey, my then editor at "i-D" about how to move the magazine from the 80s into the 90s, and wanted to make an editorial shift towards more social and environmental issues

which were beginning to enter the public arena. We spent our time discussing putting the world to rights. I'd been reading up on Gaia and earth consciousness and we talked about corporations becoming more socially responsible. Doug asked me to join Esprit as their European creative director, making me an offer to put in 100% commitment into Esprit, which I couldn't refuse.
For the next eighteen months I was constantly travelling between home, the Esprit headquarters in Düsseldorf, Milan and Paris. I worked with Doug and his art director in San Francisco, Yagi Tamotsu. It was a novel idea at the time to use a fashion company to spread a political message. Within a year we had shifted their packaging from plastic to recycled stock. but many of the ideas Doug wanted to include got vetoed by his business manager. The "Think Before You Buy" label strategy was more than they could take! Doug quit and sold his stake to launch the Deep Ecology Foundation. But the company missed his passion and energy. In those last six months of working for Esprit the internal politics gradually ground me down. I was pleased with the back view concept for the poster campaign photographed with Peggy Serota and tried to push through the campaign called, "If you could change the world what would you do", but I quit before I could get involved in its execution. Esprit ran the campaign globally for the next few years.
The underlying concept of Esprit, and the attitude to life which Doug aimed to promote were certainly inspirational and he remains someone for whom I have a lot of respect.

While I was at Esprit, I got called by UPU, the publishers of "Esquire" in Japan, saying that after two years of consumer research, they'd chosen "i-D" to be their next Japanese venture, and were we interested? I agreed with the proviso I could train and work with a Japanese art department. So I went straight from Esprit to making monthly trips to Japan.

Takashi Homma, photographer: "My first job with Terry was the cover of the first issue of 'i-D Japan'. I took five or six rolls of film of a Japanese girl singer. The Japanese staff said, please take more rolls, but Terry used the first shot from the first roll. I was really impressed."

In 1995 Junko Wong, my agent at CWC in Tokyo, contacted me. Nagase Masatoshi, famous for his part in Jim Jarmusch's movie "Mystery Train", had married Kyon Kyon, a mega-super-pop-star in Japan who featured on the first cover of "i-D Japan". He liked the cover style, and wanted me to art direct his CD and a book. I had an idea inspired by a paparazzi photo of Warhol, taken in the 70s which I'd seen while I was at "Vogue". I wanted to create a "mystery celeb in disguise in London" shoot. I had Nagase fitted with a blond wig and Kevin Davies and Jeremy Murch photographed static portraits and paparazzi-style reportage. Everyone was happy with the results, but the story reversed. My design assistant, Kumiko Kawaguchi devoted hours of work to making changes. Keiko, of CWC, was caught in the middle. We finally got the book to the printer, but the spontaneity of the camera flash was a long forgotten memory.

Caroline Baker, fashion editor and stylist: "I first met Terry Jones just before the two sevens clash year of 1977. Beatrix Miller, the editor of British 'Vogue', invited me to produce fashion stories and Terry Jones was the art director. I didn't survive there very long, I was dismissed as a punk because my stories were too street-wise for the then upper-class snobbish attitudes that dominated British 'Vogue'. I heard from Terry when he was launching a new magazine, 'i-D', and was happy to help so I contributed monthly. Terry was a great editor, encouraging you to approach your stories, and respond to fashion movements and happenings, without any editorial restraints. I was able to work with new photographers who were just making their reputations, like Robert Erdmann and Eamonn McCabe. There would be some kind of a theme for every issue which we could all interpret our own way. It was a great environment to work in and one which I have never encountered anywhere else in my career as a fashion editor."

"i-D" has always gone below the surface of dress. Fashion can and should be fun, an enjoyable outward expression of the self or of a hidden identity. "i-D" has encouraged people to think, and take a wide interest in different aspects of life by keeping an open mind and giving space to alternative and marginal viewpoints. Through it I want to give people the confidence to think that what they feel right wearing, is right for them.

"Not Another Punk Book" wasn't about fashion or clothes either. It's the people who wear the clothes that I'm

interested in. That goes back to my art college days when they tried to throw me out, simply because I looked like a painter and not a graphic designer.

People are often sorted into pigeon-holes and treated like packages. As an antidote young people create fashion which is unacceptable to society, because they don't want to be framed within the establishment. As fashions gradually become accepted by adult society, the young will invent more radical variations to express their resistance, and the instability of their class and status. But you can't recognise a person's identity just by looking at their clothes, that's why we invented the straight-up, which combined a photograph and a questionnaire.

Moichi Kuwahara, club entrepreneur: "Around 1982, Yuki Maekawa dropped into my club Pithecanthropus, and took a little picture of me that appeared in 'i-D' as a straight-up. I was very embarrassed. But Terry would say, we only have to live honestly even if we feel embarrassed at times. Since there are as many personalities as the number of human beings, we can get along peacefully if each of us understands that. And I agree with him.

Terry then went on to work with me at Club King, he provided a wonderful design solution to my idea. I don't think any club has yet risen above the concept of The Bank. The point is that if you sincerely trust the determined concept, however strange the idea looks, you trust each other also."

Understanding people by listening and learning from other cultures makes life infinitely more enjoyable. All life is unique and too precious to destroy. The "i-D" philosophy is to promote greater tolerance and global awareness, and "i-D Japan" was a lesson in understanding.

With a translator and a Japanese personal assistant, Hiromi, I travelled to Japan one week each month for sixteen month. Working five days, 18-20 hours, through translators was tough and stretched my stress levels especially as the culture of Japanese commercial publishing, research and design contrasted to all my previous experience.

Working in Japan is a total re-education, which I hope has since benefited my work. My first lesson was that "OK" does not necessarily mean "OK", black may be white but trust goes two ways and is essential for positive results.

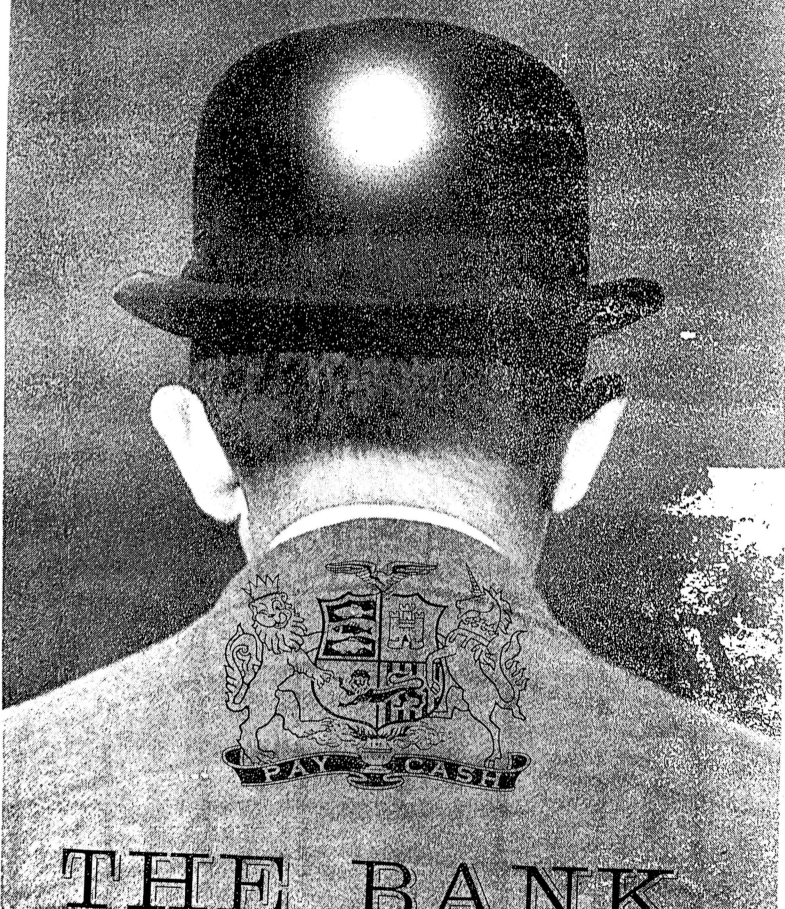

PAY CASH

THE BANK

10000

397598449

Banknote

10000

1

239759844 9

Banknote

1000000

"I prefer to ad lib, often on the deadline.     Contradiction is part of the process, questioning a

re-adjusting. Lateral thinkers are essential, telepathic lateral thinkers get the job!".

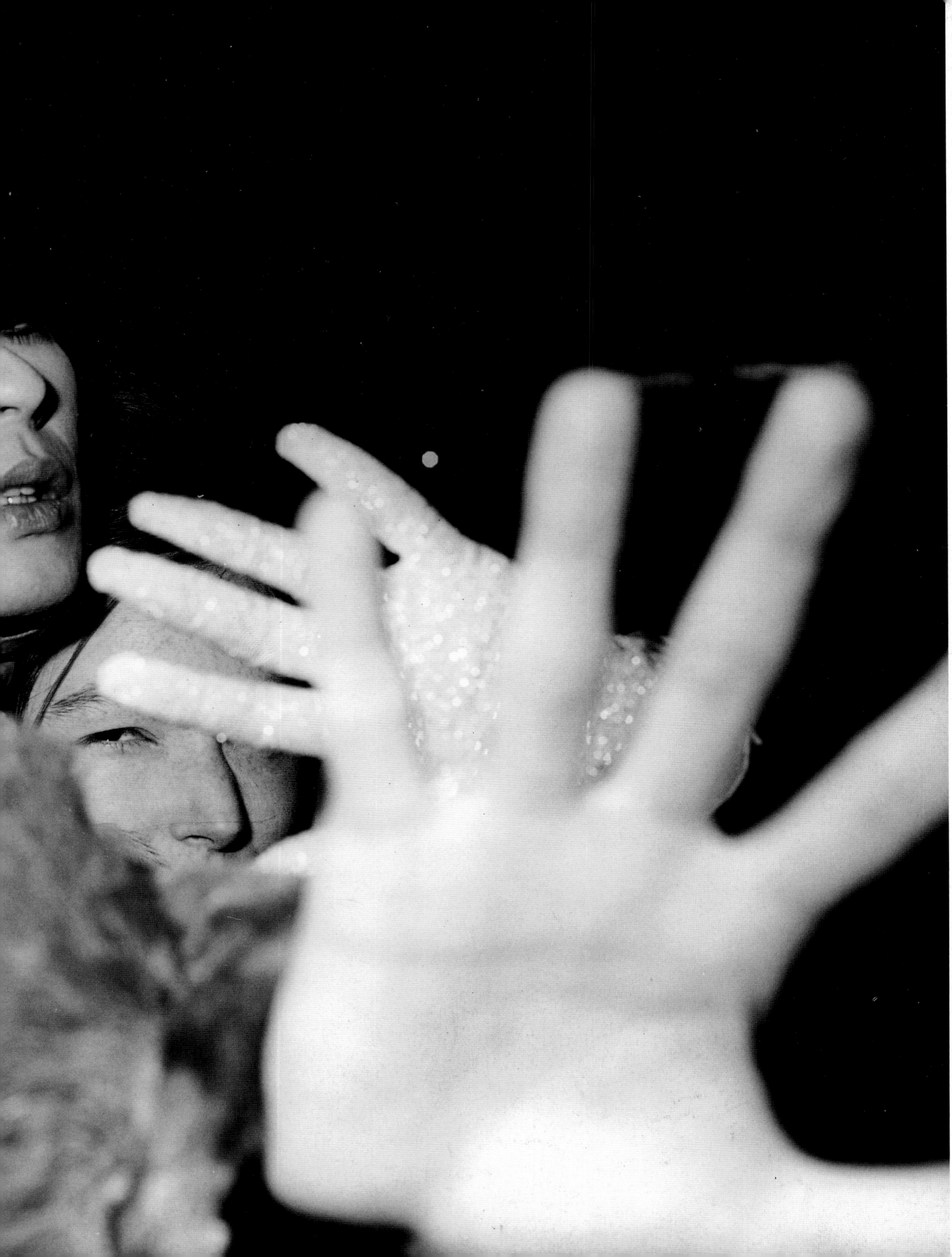

Cover image for Nagase Masatochi's CD ph. Jeremy Murch

Spreads from the Nagase Masatoshi catalogue Art Book of Vending Machine. I based the logo for the CD on his initials **NM**, as they were in the centre of the alphabet. The woodtype alphabet was made at Alan Kitchin's Type workshop. The anti-baby condom vending machine was photographed in a Munich toilet.

1x1 DM     2x1 DM

# Vending Ma-SCENE

## ART BOOK OF VENDING MACHINE
## MASATOSHI NAGASE

Nagase Masatoshi Art Book Ph.Kevin Davies Cover of first issue of i-D Japan featuring Kyon Kyon, who is married to Nagase Masatoshi ph. Takashi Homma

# i-D

## i-D JAPAN
### I-DEAS. FASHION. CLUBS. MUSIC. PEOPLE

FOR THE POLITICIANS OF THE FUTURE

アイディー・ジャパン 380yen

10月号

創刊号

THE IDENTITY ISSUE ● de la soul ++ deee lite ++ colin wilson ++ a.fujimori ++ etc.

「ホントはネ、読んで
なかったの、ライ麦畑」
KYON²

ついに！
貴花田
発覚！か

アラーキー、レニー・クラヴィッツを独占撮写！

スチャダラパー ビートたけし × ヨシキ フリッパーズ・ギター

スキャンダル

**personal**

DENDA AKEMI／24歳　双子座　A型　東京都出身。自分の足をもっている人間が、自分の足で立とうとしないような考え方は嫌い。毎日、自問自答する。疲れたら休む。本当は何も考えていないのが本音かもしれない。PHOTO BY SACHIO ONO

自分の服を探せ

i-Dent

ty Fashion

i-D
hidden

前を覚えていられる？顔は覚えていられる？顔と人とがつながっているかどうか。ホントにたくさんのバリエーションが生まれている。自分らしさというよりはずっと深いところにある。その人らしさってやつが。つまり他の人とはちがう独特の何かが。工場では作れないような神秘がそこにある。権力と地位の後ろめたさをふりおとせ。自分自身の新しいアイデアを作り出せ。

リチャード・ロング／地球を歩きながらアートを創り出す人 46歳 イギリス出身。顔は知られたくない。ただひとつ大切なのは自分の作品だから。自分がしゃべることや、外観、自分が誰であるのかなんてことは、どうでもいい。（右下の作品：Richard Long Walking in circles in Hayward Gallery) PHOTO BY TERRY JONES

秀美
血液型AB型 熊本県出身

瀬脇 郷子
22歳 水瓶座 血液型B型 鹿児島県出身

小野 幸生
28歳 双子座 O型 高知県出身

# PUBLIC Image LTD

STILL OLNY 90P

TUSRDAY SEPTEMBER 31 1978     VIRGIN VS 228

## The girls who drove me to tea, by Donut's wife Carol

O Carol     Donut

FROM DARLING MARGE our Romance Editor

**PUBLIC IMAGE**

You never listened to a word that I said
You only seen me for the clothes that I wear
Or did the interest go so much deeper
It must have been the colour of my hair
Public Image   Public Image

What you wanted was never made clear
Behind the image was ignorance and fear
You hide behind his public machine
Do you still follow the same old schemes?
Public Image   Public Image

Two sides to every story so somebody
    had to stop me
Im not the same as when I began
I will not be treated as property
Public Image   Public Image

Two sides to every story
So somebody had to stop me
Im not the same as when I began
Its not a game of monopoly
Public Image   Public Image

The Public Image you got what you wanted
The Public Image belongs to me
Its my entrance
My own creation
My grand finale
My goodbye

© PUBLIC IMAGE LTD

**No one's innocent except us..**

By RONNIE RUNNER

**Don't panic— get advice**

True story O.D.

### Refused to play Russian Roulette

**THE HAIRY MONSTER YOU LOVE TO WAKE UP WITH—See Centre Pages**

lyrics used by kind permission of the writers and Warner Brothers Music Ltd 1978

---

# PUBLIC Spot
## PIL STARTS STORM

PUBLIC IMAGE LTD
PHOTOGRAPHS COPYRIGHT ZEBULON
THURSDAY SEPTEMBER 31 1978

By JOHN GRAY Snide Correspondent

## CHAMP
### Now comes his world title bid

### DONUTS IN DEMAND

PRINTED & PUBLISHED BY PUBLIC IMAGE LTD.     *Virgin*

### Cowboy song

A MUST for all good Boy Scouts and Campfire Cowboys.

### 'I WANT TO BE WICKED' says CAROL

**REVEIL ALL ON SALE NOW**

A ZEBULON PRODUCTION ©1978. ALL PHOTOGRAPHS BY DENNIS MORRIS.

---

**Thursday September 31.** One day I had one day to make the sleeve for PIL's first single. Together with Dennis Morris we thought we could wrap the 7 inch vinyl single in that day's newspaper, like fish and chips. So I picked up a **Daily Mirror** and that became the format. We just changed the headlines around and censored out some of the text. The image in the centre-fold was a giant phallic sculpture lifted off my studio wall from another one-off magazine idea, called picturepaper.

---

PUBLIC IMAGE LIMITED

### high-speed hours in the life of the world's fastest

# HAIRY MONSTER WITH A FIVE-TO-NINE JOB..

Vera Dangerous YOU can pick her up on any street corner and in any bar DON'T TAKE THE CHANCE

ADVERTISEMENT

"I was wild with my chopper **PiL** until I discovered"

'It's the days after mornings like this that are the worst'

CENSORED

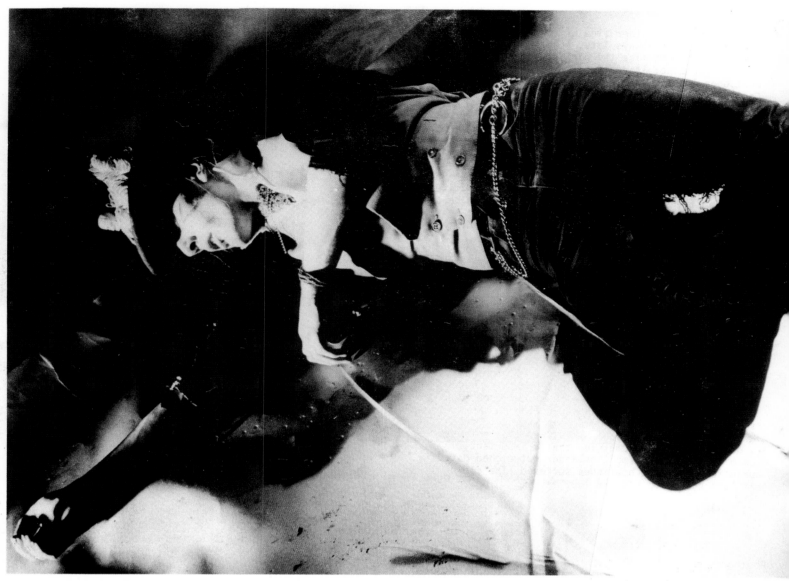

Spread from i-D No. 1 Steve New ph. Brian Griffin with censored interview.
1962, my first experience of censoring text. This is a spread from the college magazine which I edited.
As the college had just received diploma status I had to censor the word "bullshit" to avoid being kicked out.

## "What is an Art College?"

Graphics are marks

These marks
may be signs
    (letters of the alphabet) →(words)

and/or images

Designing graphics means

making
or choosing relevant marks
    and/or images

and organising them
to effect a positive response
in the observer

Painting is a special kind of Graphics,
but a painter controls what his work says,
the designer does not. He is concerned with how
a given message is communicated

# CONFiDE

STEVE NEW---HIDING HIS I.D.

What are you wearing-from top to bottom?
"The hat ~~something I begged,something I stole,something I borrowed~~.Nothing that I have on now is mine.Well it is mine n-
ow,because I stole it!" ~~stole this,stole the wa-~~
istcoat!"
Yeah?
"It goes with the jacket... ~~fucking~~ art piece...stole the so-
cks,nicked the shoes-stealing and nicking is different.Steal-
ing is from somebody you know,nicking is from somebody you d-
ont ~~and you fucking swipe it.~~
What about the ostrich feather?
"A gift,a feather is always a gift".
A feather symbolises gifts?

It doesn't symbolise gifts...well ~~it does~~ in a way...it symbolises my remains, ~~which~~ at this point ~~are down to a fucking~~
minimum. ~~My remains,what remains of me now.~~ I'm a composite of
rags,this mans an amalgamation of junk,which could be ambig-- ~~uous~~"

Even this a 22 carat scarf?
"Oh yeah a 22 carat scarf... nicked,not stolen,nicked."
An investment?
"No way!I havn't got any money.. ~~how do I wear clothes?Aah~~
~~Busty Egan.~~ I haven't been into a boutique for about 2'yrs
~~and~~ I don't care,I don't notice what people wear. ~~Except what~~ it
all looks ~~pretty much~~ black n'white these days,girls look
just-like boys now.I've ~~got~~ no time for clothes."

"It's ~~really like~~ poxy 'cause all they do is make people
think of whats outside ~~them when~~ they should be thinking of
what's inside.Most people haven't got anything inside when
they walk around in clothes-including me.Why do I wear clothes?
    To hide..."

P.T.O. for S.N. in Con-.................

Chipie campaign ph. Brian Griffin Stylist Simon Foxton
While we were photographing in France, Tricia, the producer, found a local French teenager who could
bend at ridiculous angles. The Ritz Hotel allowed us to take a shot in their tea-room because I had made a
book about the hotel. The baby was in the cafe were we had lunch.

Lürzer, Conrad

# BLUE POOL

edition hat es sich zur Aufgabe gemacht, Sie Monat für Monat mit einer neuen Farbe zu begeistern.

Hier sehen Sie Blue Pool, den wasserfesten Cream Eye Shadow.

Dieses kühle Blau ist von tiefer Leuchtkraft und läßt Ihre Augen strahlen.

Passend dazu gibt es den neuen wasserfesten Super Lash Mascara.

edition erhalten Sie im autorisierten Fachgeschäft. Auch in Österreich.

## edition
cosmetics

*Geschminkt mit Blue Pool Cream Eye Shadow und Super Lash Mascara Waterproof Black Mustang 80. edition cosmetics, eine Division der Margaret Astor AG.*

1978, Michael Conrad asked me to work on advertising in his agency. I didn't want to do fashion but he got me working with him on cigarettes, shavers, politics and make up - Blue Pool was one of the Margaret Astor ads. produced in 1978/79

Dans la photo,
le pantalon
modèle "Beyrouth"
New York Industrie,
plus simplement
connu comme
"modèle New York":
le pantalon le plus
vendu au monde
après le jean,
copies comprises.

TON PANTALON !

le CONTRACEPTIF le plus sûr

alberto biani pour NEW YORK industrie

Sondini & Giuseppe Europa • A.D. Terry Jones • Ph. Thomas Degen

194

COSÌ FAN TUTTE

alberto biani
per
NEW YORK

Without "problems" myself, and most other creative people, would be out of a job. Sometimes it helps to create problems so I'll invent difficulties as part of the creative process. Like when I asked a popular Japanese band to cross the road during rush hour on the busiest intersection in Tokyo, when the traffic had the right of way, while we photographed them for "i-D Japan". How we define and solve problems creates the end result. Collaborating with people whose positive energy goes towards a solution is my ideal working environment and I've been fortunate to work with loads of talented people. Through choosing clients like Fiorucci, Willy Bogner, Chipie, Mexx, and Doug Tompkins at Esprit, the network of partnerships has become global. Michael Conrad, who has an advertising agency, Lurzer/Conrad in Frankfurt, saw the first and second issues of "Sportswear International", and invited me for a brainstorming session. I remember telling him that I had quit British "Vogue" and would love to work on anything that wasn't "frocks". The collaboration with a young art director at Lurzer/Conrad, Franz Aumueller, produced a lasting friendship. Ten years later he was approached by Greg and Claudia, who worked for the agency Avant Garde, and later formed .Start, to find an art director for their client Fire and Ice, Willy Bogner's active clothing line. At that time I was working with Zebulon which was a partnership with Dennis Morris, the photographer I collaborated with on record sleeve designs. We have the same birth sign and as he is from Jamaica we called ourselves Zebulon,

which is the Rastafarian name for Virgo. I signed the artwork packages for Zebulon design work, with a big "Z", anonymously just like a "graphic design Zorro".
Franca Soncini, fashion advertiser, Milan: "My idea is to be a catalyst between my clients' needs and the artist's creative process, and fully respect their professional roles. This means always having the possibility to reconsider concepts, explore new solutions, exchange ideas and feelings in what is, and remains until the very final moments, a work-in-progress. And this is exactly what happened working with Terry. What seemed fundamental five minutes before could be done away with ten minutes later, if we felt that a more interesting and satisfying idea was unexpectedly coming up. Because it is only when you are freed from fixed schemes and preconceived solutions that results can be truly innovative and carry your distinctive mark."

Lorenzini shirts campaign, the first collaboration with Franca Soncini who became a mentor and friend. This catalogue was photographed in 1986 by Robert Erdmann, with the young David Sims assisting. Stylist Caroline Baker.

CARINNE: Chain bracelets from Butler and Wilson and Cobra. Brown and black world print, skimpy top and black and white map of the world print both by Body Map available from Harrods Way-In, Jones Kings Rd and Floral St and Hudson and Hudson 71 St Mary St Cardiff. Unlaced bovver boots from Office Shoes at Hyper Hyper, Kensington High St. Black jacket by Azzedine Alaïa at Joseph pour la maison.

Silk undies by Katharine Hamnett tied in a knot available from Katharine Hamnett shops Kings Rd and South Molton St, Equasion Bristol, Steel Notts, Otokio 3 South Anne St Dublin. (For other clothes details see Brad)

VANISHING ACT-ion

44

HAIR AND MAKE-UP BY WILLIAM FALKNER. SHOT AT LIPSTICK STUDIOS.

MODELS AKURE FROM LOOK, BRAD HARRYMAN FROM MARCO RASALA, LENE FROM MODELS 1, CARINNE FROM PREMIER AND BETH FROM PREMIER.

198

Love Bites ~~Back~~ Black

1st    1ST

Martine wears: Rayon rounded lapels black jacket: Yohji Yamamoto, 22 Brompton Arcade, SW1. Matador's hat: John Burke, 20 Pembridge Rd. W11. Dalmation dog: Brats, 624c Fulham Road, London SW6. Fob watch: Brats, 624c Fulham Road, SW6.

Martine wears: Moleskin black vest: Yohji Yamamoto, 22 Brompton Arcade, London SW1. Chisel-toe black shoes: Toby Anderson for Agent (tel 727 8321). Stockings: Emanuel from Dept. stores. Sunglasses and watches from a selection at Brats, 624c Fulham Road, SW6.

Fashion by Joe McKenna. Photography by Robert Erdman. Model Martine at Marco Rasala. Hair by Valmar. Make-up by Carol Langbridge.

32

i-D THE DANGEROUS ISSUE 69

Chris from Brixton, found patrolling Method Air. Wears: short sleeve zip T-shirt £48 by Hamnett Active available from the Hamnett Active unit at Fusion and stockists nationwide.

Liam was discovered working at the Vintage magazine shop, hangs out anywhere from Dance Wicked to Subterania. Wears: Big 'E' jacket £60 by Levi's and original '40s 501s £90 both from Rokit; and nylon shirt £48 by Hamnett Active available from the Hamnett Active unit at Fusion and stockists nationwide.

FASHION BY MELANIE WARD
PHOTOGRAPHY BY DAVID SIMS
HAIR BY GUIDO
MODEL TOM BOWEN AT TAKE TWO
SHOT AT CLICK STUDIO (071-00 0121) AND
THE MARQUEE, CHARING CROSS ROAD, LONDON WC2

Customised lace top from Paradiso
Bodyworks, 41 Old Compton Street,
London W1; trousers by Helmut Lang
from Joseph, 77 Fulham Road SW3 and
Kafka, 41 Union Terrace, Aberdeen;
fingerless studded gloves from Carnaby
Street, London W1.

# for real

Pop trash meets rock'n'roll sleaze. Let's make some noise!

Black cotton cable knot cardigan, Black viscose zip skirt both by Joseph Tricot 18 Sloane Street SW1 and 16 South Molton Street W1. Pale pink linen slip by Goldie Lingerie from Harrods Way in and Ferrante of Wimbledon. Black Strappy T-shirt by Katharine Hamnett from Joseph's Chinese Laundry South Molton Street and King's Road. SW3. Stockings and suspenders throughout by Aristoc from selected stores.

i-D February 1986 ph. Robert Erdmann Stylist Amanda Grieve, the white background looked too clean, so we created an off-set background from an early Landscape issue of i-D

Black linen zip from dress
by Parachute from Liber-
ty Regent Street W1, and
Hudson and Hudson, Car-
diff
Black mohair jacket by
Katharine Hamnett from
The Chinese Laundry.

43

like my expectations to be surpassed".

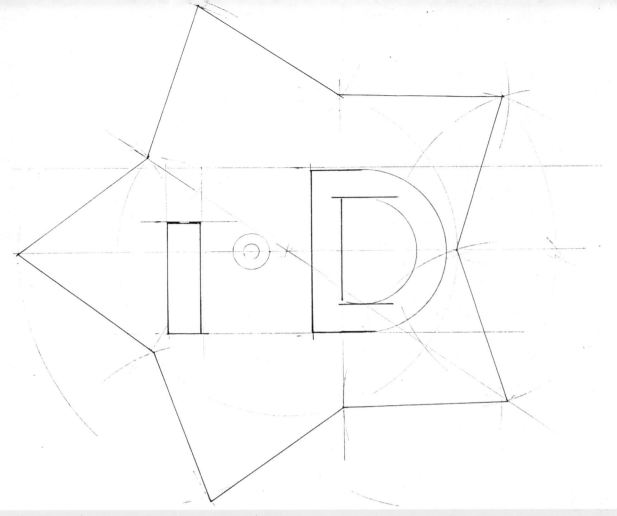

James Palmer

SANDIE. Mode; wearing Williwear clothes. Hair Vidal Sasoon student. Make-up self, blusher Mary Quant, Christian Dior eye liner & mascara necklace Rosita pearls 1961 from Alders of Croydon, leg warmers Gamba, Beauchamp Place, Shoes Gamba. Sometimes likes London, likes N.Y. Music: blues, jazz, some reggae. Goes to a mixture of places, quite likes Coconut Grove & Chicago pizza place.

JONATHAN. Mode: American and models in Japan. Clothes, T shirt, trousers & socks all athletic from America. Shoes & hat from Worlds End. Feet shown below.

JOSE & MADELAINE. MADELAINE. Mode: Floris hair by herself, jacket from Johnsons £l Jumper from Johnsons £4. Likes: Rockabill Meteors, T.O.H., Deltas, buying records. Dislikes: disco freaks, punk, funk, soul boys. JOSE. Mode: works as a cleaner in a hospital. Hair by Fred's of Brighton (se issue 6). Jacket from Johnsons Kings Road t-shirt from Eastbourne £2.50. Likes & dislikes the same as Madelaine.

200

ITEM 2100    SEX GANG CHILDREN

GAIL:Designer for Playboy. Outfit by Ya Ya. Likes to shock people with clothes,"I think that"s important, I'm always impressed by interestingly dressed people" "The only thing I couldn't manage without is my music and for that I go to Batcave, Studio 21 and Gullivers on futurist nights." Survival on the dole;"I managed by not eating."

PHOTO BY STEVE JOHNSTON

PHOTO BY NICK KNIGHT

Dave Roberts.Shoes free. Jeans free from Julie.Belt free from another girlfriend.Shirt free from a girl after my house burned down."T-shirt from Julie Jewellery rose earring from Julie bangle and chains 10p each from Brixton market.Music;Soft Cell "Martin", Hanna Shugulla, "Lici Marleen",The Doors, Southern Death Cult,Cori Josias "Straight Down the Line"(White label).Likes George a Romesro films, B'movies, sex films,cheap horror films, Derek Jarmans "Jubilee" and others. Dislikes "Cultures think- ing they are more important than other cultures." Born 25/1/'60 in Nairobi, Kenya. Books; JG Ballard (everything),Lautremont, Verlaine and EE Cummings.Interests outside the band;"My solo band 'The Carcrash International' and a solo LP "The Whip" released in March on Camera."

Terry born 1960 in Tronto.Boots from army shop,Trousers Jumble sale,Beret nicked army surplus T-shirt from fans.Baubles aquired Dislikes people who say doing things ween they won't,rock and roll,wasps. Likes cities especially city parks, Cinema, arguments and nasty surreal- ists.Bands Simple Minds, Soft Cell, Psychic TV,Death Cult, Gun Club and Blood and Roses.Favourite reads; Charles Budowski, Kenneth Grant, people who've been to hell.

Selection

en appear una
rily attached to
Thus it is rendere
ugh natural selecti
metimes the case; c
other sex, as comn
s on what I have ca
depends, not on a st
anic beings or to exter
en the individuals of o
ssession of the other se
ssful competitor, but few
efore, less rigorous than na
gorous males, those whic
ture, will leave most pro
ends not so much on g
ons, confined to the ma
would have a poor ch
l selection, by always
ly give indomitable
to the wing to strik
nner as does the br
his best cocks. How
descends, I know
ghting, bellowing,
ce, for the posse-
n observed fighti

James Palmer

KATE. Mode: i-D Cover girl (issue 7). Photoed at Cha Chas Tuesday eve. Trousers Sweet Charity £18, braces borrowed, t-shirt Du Du, Finchley Road, £6, Shoes Sasha £12, hat from some bazaar in India.

JOEY & JULIE. Mode:
JOEY: Hair self & Julies mum, jacket bleached, boots Bracknell Mkt.
JULIE: Hair my mum, jkt. & boots Bracknell Mkt. They are from Ascot, they like to go to Waterloo & just doss around. Like: 4 Skins, Meteors & Angelic Upstarts. Love: shagging. Reading F.C. for the top of the League but Julie supports Chelsea. Like: to go to gigs and that with the Ascot Barmy Army, they go beserk, pogo & spit. Like: the Queen.

TRIFFIC!

DE LUXE SHOES. Mode: Run by Tim Poultney & Joe O'Connor at 402 Kings Road, Worlds End, Chelsea SW10. Joe started a shop 4 years ago in Beaufort Market called 'Perverts' and when it closed opened Xstremes in Liverpool, 56 Stanley Street (051-236 0289), stocking the best of current fashion. They then opened in the Ken. Mkt with t-shirts, accessories etc. and now back to the Worlds End opposite Beaufort Market with De Luxe Shoes. They feature a wide range of shoes with an even wider range of colour combinations and an original decor. New styles in at the end of May: thigh boots in black patent, broderie anglais white booties, canvas flat shoes plus many others. De Luxe shoes are also available from their Liverpool branch. Featured in pic: Black suede flat shoe with bow £15.50. Red leather bootie with black

PHOTOS BY STEVE JOHNSTON

ITEM 2150 TITS AND ARSE

and Jinny, And1: Sex Gang, Children. es Walters/Herzog/Roeg films,"Seb- ians" by Derek Jarman and Klaus ski "He has such an expressive e, Charlie Chaplin, who's a genius, kues Brel, Edith Piaf, Elvis, eries tea room, Thundercrack, Picasso, tic art, red stockings and vaseline. s: Soft Cell, Southern Death t, The Venuonettes, Dislikes n Hillbillies, apathy, drugs and n again Christians, Hair Andys, Brix- "I dye it myself,"Coat Sadies k shop £2, Boots Brixton Mkt £1. ny, Hat: jumble sale 10p, jacket well. Skirt made by a friend. es from Glasgow 15p

SUE CLOWES. Designer. Hair self styled. Clothes next summers collection - dungerees £35 T-shirt £12 (they're called 'Dollymops') Boots Freeds £75. Likes TV AND Fast food. Dislikes Taxi drivers and wire coat hangers, "At college I wasn't really into fashion - I preferred printing and getting my hands dirty. Prints will always be popular, there are so many possibilities to use. Like at the moment I'm working on a more subtle approach the Derore Method. I'm burning in the patterns with acid then adding ink which expands to look blotchy and bleed when you print it - I hate perfection in print. The inspirations for my summer collection are based around Haymarket prostitutes in Victorian times - women who were stronger than men and manipulated them. The look is glamorous but scruffy, like being dragged through a hedge backwards in

# a. art teazers!

Art should inspire thought to provoke conversation, so here we present some recent talking points. From painters to cartoonists, performance artists to zazous, Ron Arad to Cecil Gee, Michael Clark to The Kooky Shop – i-D brings you the very latest Art check-outs. Inwardly digest!!

funk art

Background:
Portrait head of Yhassstone, found in a tomb at Gizeh, made about 2700 B.C. Presently in Vienna, Kunsthistorisches Museum.

# WORLDWIDE MANUAL OF STYLE

the art issue

i-D MAGAZINE No. 28 AUGUST 1985  £1.00

# i-D

the indispensable document
of fashion style & ideas

LET's DANCE!

baroque 'n' roll!

5 013071 000065

# i-D

SHOCK
HORROR
FILTH
FURY

OUT ALREADY

Cover of i-D No. 10 featuring art editor Moira Bogue ph. Steve Johnston, graphically manipulated. From an sx 70 polaroid.

£1

# i-D

**FLASH
CRASH
SPLASH
N'DASH**

*WET 'n' WILD*

Cover i-D No. 12 ph. Steve Johnston. We asked the singer with the Sex Beatles to stand on a roof with a pan of water thrown in her face for each shot. She braved it out for a roll of 36 shots, for the Wet'n'wild issue

# MAN

Photo by Thomas Degen

ADAM and EVE: Unemployed.Clothes: Adam
wears a fig leaf whoch he picks fresh
every day. Eve wears only long hair, Adams
hair cut by Eve. Likes: Apple trees and
clever snakes. Dislikes: Angels with burning
swords. They think navels are just a
fashion among the young people which is going
to disappear sooner or later. What do they
think about the future? "Blood,Sweat
and Tears"

**ACT ONE:**
*In the garden of Eden.Eve offers Adam the forbidden fruit.*
*Adam is hesitant.*

EVE: "DIVE IN,DIVE IN,DIVINE....STRAP ON A TAIL AND COMMENCE.'"

ADAM:(speaking with his mouth full) "THE FUTURE ONLY EXISTS THROUGH LIFE. I WANT TO FOLLOW MY DESTINY AND CHEAT MY FATE."

EVE: "WITH WORDS YOU CAN SNEAK AROUND-LOOKS SPEAK FOR THEMSELVES....'"

VOICE IN THE SKY: (enraged) " IDEAS HAVE VIRILITY LIKE GERMS. YOU ARE DEALING WITH PSYCHIC EPIDEMICS'"

EVE: "BUT RHYTHM AND STYLE DANCE HAND IN HAND."

ADAM: "IN THE BEGINNING THERE WAS BIG BEAT..."

EVE: "SEX AND SWEAT IS BEST YOU BET"

V.I.S:(livid) OUT! NOW! (they leave)

ADAM: "WE WILL PLAY SPIRITUAL ROBINSON CRUSOE FOR A WHILE YET."

EVE: "YEAH,WELL YOU HAVE TO EXPEND SOME ENERGY TO GET RESULTS..."

ANTHROPOLOGIST: (emerging from bushes) "A CHILD OF FIVE COULD UNDERSTAND THIS. SEND SOMEONE TO FETCH A CHILD OF FIVE."

*CURTAIN*

Dialogue compiled from 2 and a half years of I-D gems.Special thanks
to:Ben Browton,Genesis P.Orridge,Vivien Westwood,Joly Better Badges,
Mechthild Nawiasku,Perru Haines.Alix Sharkeu and Groucho Marx.

---

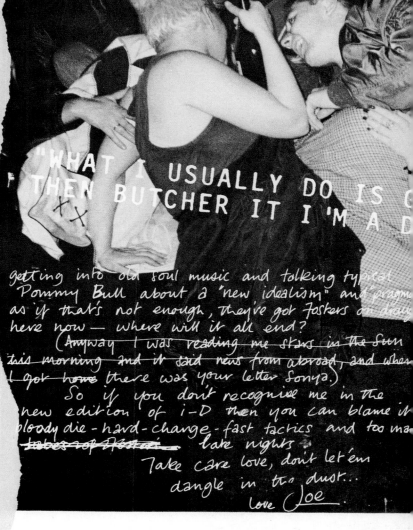

"WHAT I USUALLY DO IS
THEN BUTCHER IT I'M AD

*\* you look like a bloody lobster,love...
about using cheap suntan oil.*

27, TRULOCKE GDNS.,
EARLS COURT
LONDON S.W.6.

Dear Sonya          Thanks for the letter and
piccy of you \* Anyway,Remember those photos I sent you
last year? Of me and Joe in our ~~trendy~~ trendy
get-up? Well things move so fast here I've damn
near bust a gut keeping me wardrobe up to date!
See, just after that piccy was taken some smart
Pom slammed on the anchors and it was all
change — "dressing down", they called it.
~~Too too when replaced clothes and clothes~~
So true to form, I ~~got me scissors out and~~
went to town, ~~nothing~~ ripped off all ~~the~~ me
sweatshirt sleeves, got the Black and Dekker
on me Levis — suddenly I realised I was here
just a few years ~~ago~~ before...Deja bloody vu!
    I mean , is there any reason for ripping
expensive clobber into holes? (some pommy arsehole
found one) ~~And~~ times are even harder with
holes in your knees and ~~your~~ yer arse hanging
out and a true-Brit winter on the way...
Even worse, countless other diggers are wearing
holey knees too — I'm in a uniform again.
    Honest love, this really confusing.
Some WAGs doing an "allnighter"-style club
~~~~ down Wardour Street...
There's this shop around the corner called
DEMOB with clothes like they wear in that film
BLADE RUNNER, no, they're even bloody funnier
than that !...There's a club called the DIRTBOX
that moves twice a bloody week... and everybody's

getting into old soul music and talking typical
Pommy Bull about a "new idealism" and "pragma
as if that's not enough, they've got Fosters on draug
here now — where will it all end?
(Anyway I was ~~reading me stars in the sun~~
~~this morning and it said news from abroad, and when~~
~~I got home~~ there was your letter Sonya.)
    So if you don't recognise me in the
new edition of i-D then you can blame it
bloody die-hard-change-fast tactics and too ma
~~lots of these~~ late nights
Take care love, don't let 'em
dangle in the dust...
                    love Joe.

Two spreads from i-D No. 10 1983. The editorial style was intended to slow down the reader and encourage the process of discovery. Until issue 13 i-D published four times a year

"PLAYGIRLS PLAY ABOUT WITH THE SEMOTICS OF FASHION IN THE SAME WAY THAT THE AWARE YOUTH OF THIS COUNTRY ARE LEARNING TO DO" Steve Blyh

## "BRAVE BABIES MUST HAVE STYLE"

NAPPY-RASH IS NOT ENOUGH... BRAVE BABIES MUST HAVE STYLE. BORN TO BE WISE, A GENERATION HAS GROWN UP WITH AN INSTINCT FOR IMAGE AND IT'S MAN IPULATION. CITY KI-DS ESPECIALLY HAVE ABSORBED A CROSS-CULTURAL EDUCATION. WITH EYES AND EARS OPEN THEY PLUNDER THEIR TRUE HERITAGE THEY LEARN THE LESSONS OF DRESS CODE AND THEN BREAK THE RULES-NEVER AGAIN WILL STYLE SEEM DISTANT STYLE WIZE OR PRECIOUS. THEY BEND-A-GENDER HERE STEAL-A-STANCE THERE... ANYTHING TO SATISFY THEIR LUST FOR LIFE.

(WINSTON KING TAKES CLASSIC FABRICS AND STRAINS THEM INTO UTILITY DESIGNS CHECK HIS PIN STRIPE BOILERSUITE ON SALE IN BEAK ST.)

AS THEY GROW THEY WANT NEW TOYS AND DEVELOPE A TASTE FOR THE THEATRICAL SIDE OF LIFE. (THEIR PRANKS ARE DOCUMENTED IN THE SCHOOL MAGAZINE INFANTILE-DISORDER) SOME GROW IMPASSIVE AND ARE NOT CONTENT WITH DELIVERING LINES THAT OTHERS INTERUPT FOR THEM. FOR THOSE WHO CHOSE TO PLAY FOR FUN RATHER THAN KEEPS, I-D CHECK OUT AN INTERESTING NEW GAME CALLED 'TRAVELLER'.

Let's pretend! Let's pretend that I am a powerful warrior and you're a clever thief who's an OK-guy roundness and Gloria's a beautiful princess who's been captured by an evil magician and held in his castle and we've got to rescue her and so we're fighting our way in through the guards. Gloria decides to get herself out of the mess she's in and lures the guard into her cell by pretending she's sick and hits him over the head with a chair and runs out of the cell and down the hall just in time to meet us as we fight our way in and we all run towards the main gate but just before we get there the magician discovers she's missing and conjures a horrible demon to stop us ...

### TRAVELLER

Imagination is the border of TRAVELLER. Three or more players are needed, one of which will act as gamesmaster, referee, or GOD. He will create the scenario and control the action. His purpose is to make the game flow, give a theme, throw in surprise elements or red herrings and generally keep the game away from the board (a star chart) and thus eliminate compacency. He may make things more difficult for the players or reward them.

The players generate their characters, by a combination of casting die and choosing certain backgrounds and qualities e.g. physical strength, intelligence, agility medical experience, marksmanship, computer operation, engineering etc.

The players also choose their own goal. The aim of a player, then, is not to wipe out all other players or finish first or end up with all the money, but to play the most interesting game while acheiving their chosen ambition.

Does this sound familiar? If not, why not?

"Traveller is a trade mark owned by Game Designers' Worship Inc, Bloomington, Illinois, U.S.A. for its science fiction role-playing game. Traveller is printed in the U.K. under licence by Games Workshop Ltd, London. The extracts above/below in this article are reprinted with permission."

"Traveller is printed in the U.K. by Games Workshop Ltd, London. It is available from games, hobby and model shops throughout the country or from Games Workshop's own shops in London, Manchester, Birmingham, Sheffield and Nottingham."

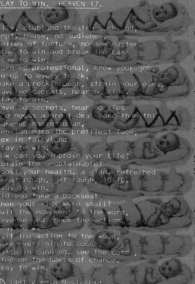

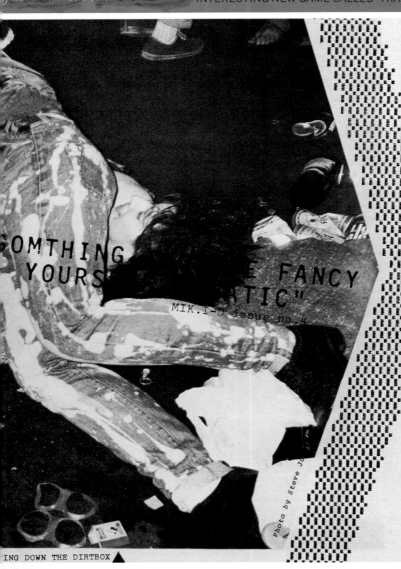

SOMTHING YOURS ...E FANCY ...TIC"
MIK. I-D issue no.4

photo by Steve Jo...

ING DOWN THE DIRTBOX ▲

MISS BINNY: Coat "Wilma. Friend. Gave it to me. Knitting: I've been doing it since I was six. Densil is one of my accessories." Likes: "Densil loves me and I love monkeys." Dislikes: "We hate pop music". "The advent of the Ruebens women **is nigh**".

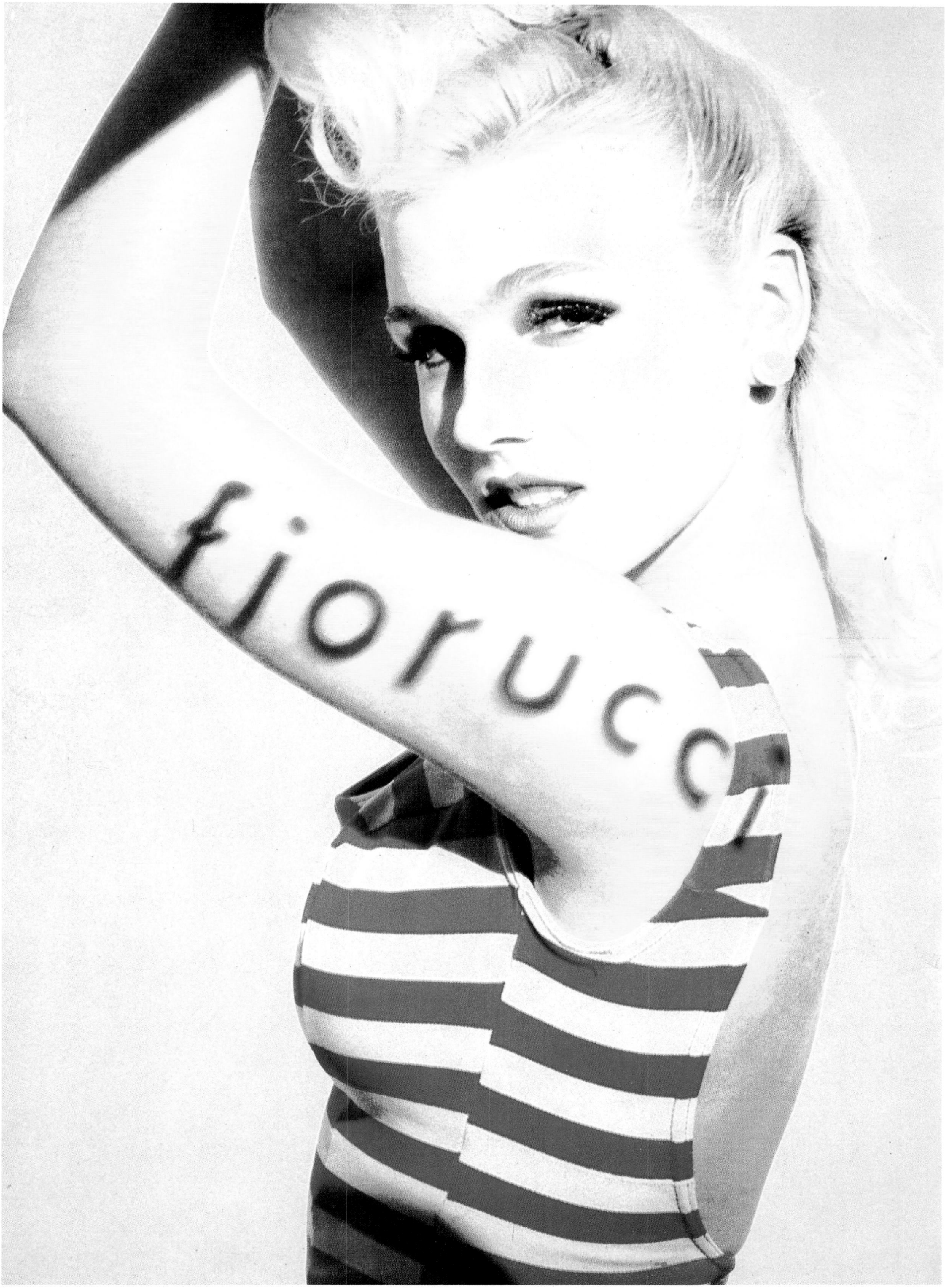
fiorucci

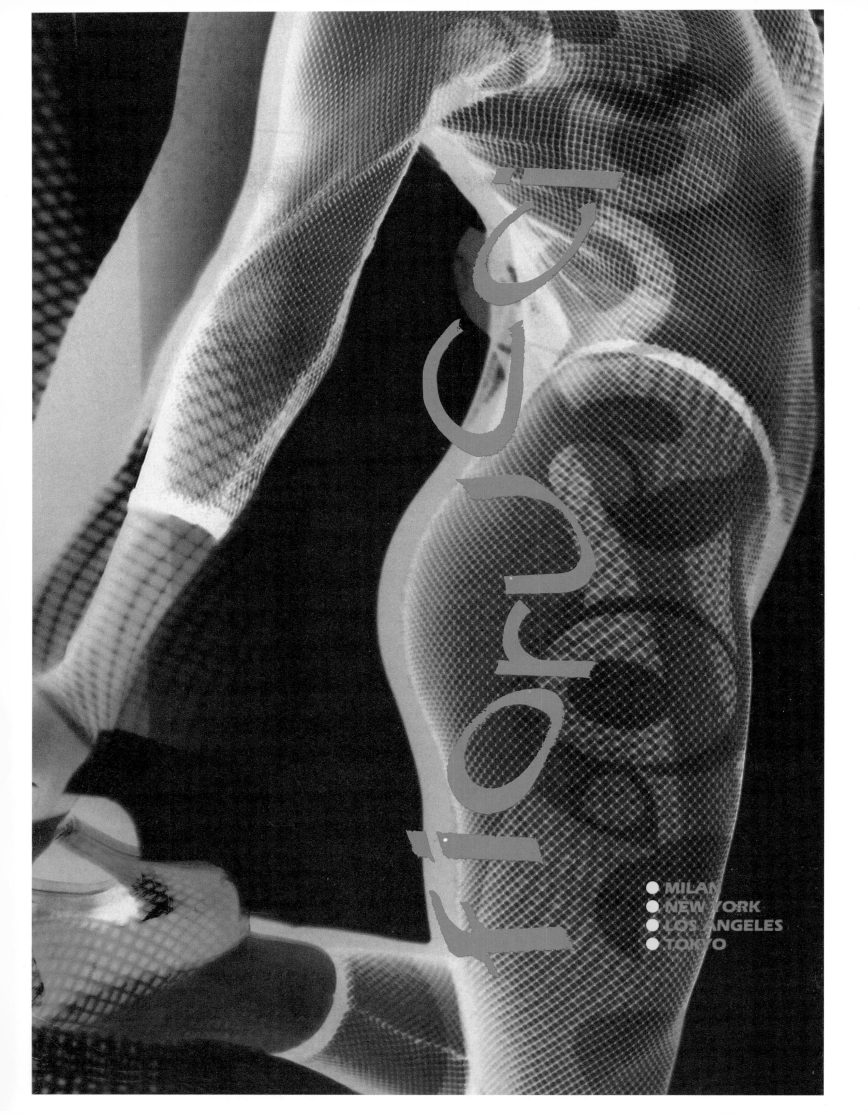

fiorucci

● MILAN
● NEW YORK
● LOS ANGELES
● TOKYO

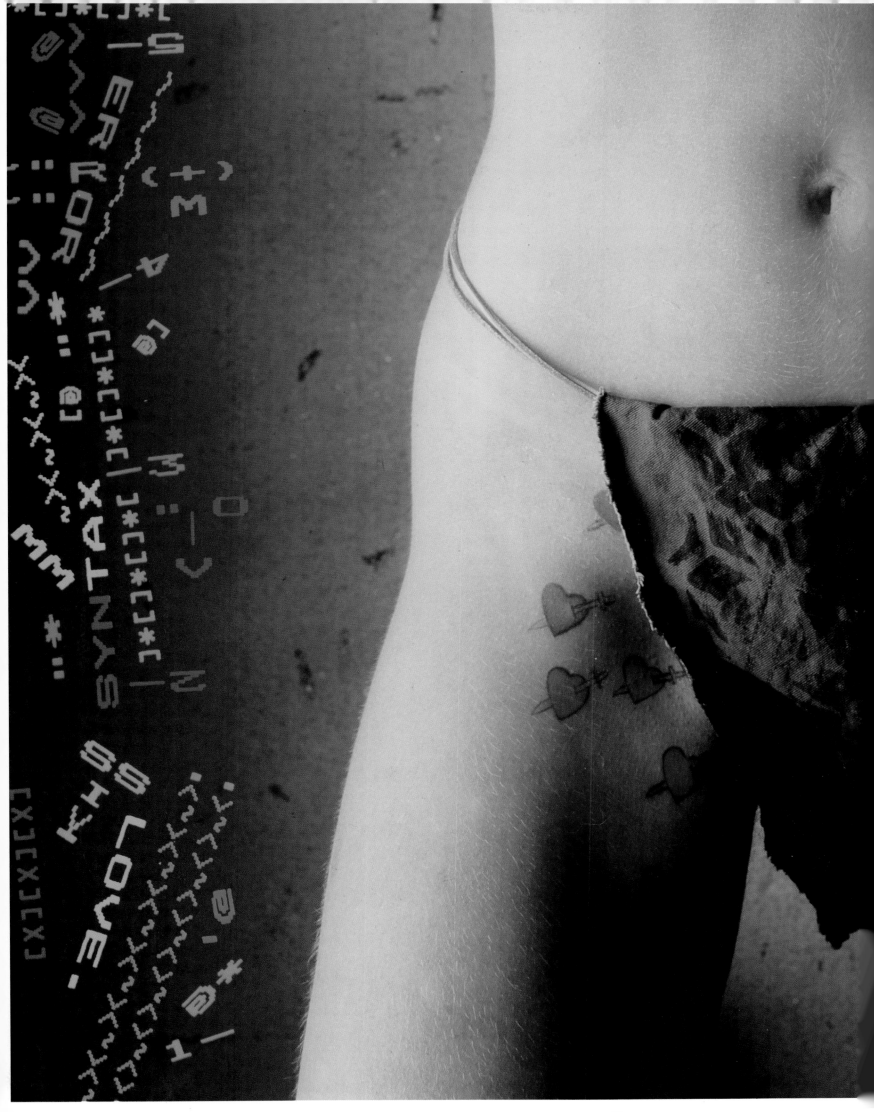

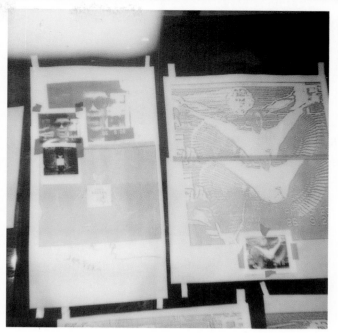

Fiorucci's Italian Rising Star exhibition, Tokyo 1986. We created an instant happening at Seibu with Hagime Tachibana manipulating video stills with a Fairlight computer

MC Merlin and Japanese rapper Tycoon To$hi

Our hosts, Club King, founded in 1987 by Moichi Kuwahara, are responsible for most of the present influx to Japan of the best Britain has to offer in the worlds of fashion, music and club culture. Within Japan itself their involvement has stretched to incorporate TV, radio, video and record production as well as merchandising and promotional tours. Plans for the future include their own record label, radio shows and video promotions. For all further details contact them at 3-7-5 Jingumae, Shibuya-Ku, Tokyo. Tel (03) 470 4392.

Jay Strongman, DJ

Sarak Stockbridge's band Choice

Roy Marsh, DJ

Watching psychedelic videos before the club opens

TOKYO! '88

i-D

The Spiral Hall Exhibition

Tim Simenon, pop star and DJ

**Suede,**
**pop group and**
**current music**
**press darlings.**
What do you want to achieve in the
next five years?
Brett Anderson, 24:
"Learn to give off the
smell of roses by the power
of thought." Bernard
Butler, 22: "To write a
string of classic, flawless
records, to acquire a
ridiculous collection of
guitars and spend as little
as possible on clothes."
Mat Osman, 24: "Sitting
in people's heads, prodding
them regularly." Simon
Gilbert, 27: "Musical
world domination."

i-D Now exhibition at the Imagination Gallery, London. Life-sized blow-up portraits included Suede ph. Wolfgang Tillmans

Eugene Souleimen, 30, hairdresser who has teased tresses for Kylie, Beatrice Dalle, Vic Reeves and Annie Lennox. What do you want to achieve in the next five years? "A balance between work and play. Make loads of money enjoying my work."

Spiral Tribe, anarchist sound system who've been rocking the travellers' raves; also recently signed a recording deal.

ホンマ タカシ、マーク・ルボン、
ウォルフガング・ティルマン、
ロナルド・ストゥープス＝写真
TAKASHI HOMMA, MARK LEBON, WOLFGANG
TILLMANS, RONALD STOOPS＝PHOTOGRAPHY
ヘレン・ミード＝取材・文
HELEN MEAD＝TEXT
石川 れい子＝翻訳

224

インスタント・インスタレ

ディレクターを務めたテリー・ジョーンズは言う。「下手すると総倒れになるくらい、いろんな材料をつめこんだ。こんなことを試みた者は今までいない。ありふれた、希望のない表現への反発として、ファッションルネッサンスを創造したかったんだ」

人気DJのトーマスとモリ

電子スチルカメラによる撮影
photo by W.T

ルーシャ（モデル兼歌手／ベロニック・リロイを着用）「愛と音楽が大切」
photo by T.H

パーティーにはヨーロッパ中のクリエイターたちがかけつけた
photo by T.H

「インスタント・インスタレーション」という名のエキシビション。それは、1月9日、イタリアのフローレンスにある17世紀に建てられた宮殿で行われた。

デザイナーやスタイリスト、モデル、カメラマンたちが、パーティー仲間を連れて、ヨーロッパ中からこのイベントのためにフローレンスにやって来た。このイベントにイロを添えたのは、テクノロジー。カメラ、ビデオ、ファクシミリ、フォトコピーによって、パーティーの模様が撮影され、ダンスフロアに次々に飾られた。カメラや電子スチルカメラで撮った写真を、すぐその場でレーザーコピアやバブルジェットプリンターで被写体の実物大に引き伸ばし、展示されたのだ。その間、ダンスフロアに流れていたのは、

ァーチャル・リアリティ・システムによる映像
photo by T.H

i-Dの表紙写真を撮影中の
ロメオ・ジリを着たモデル
photo by T.H

I-D NOW

テクノロジーで踊ろう

i-Dが100号目に達した。
もちろんUK版のハナシ。
で、100号を祝うイベントだ。
ファッションとテクノロジーとハウス。あらゆるものが
融合され、ヨーロッパ中から集まったクリエイターたちが踊った。
これは、今までにない試みのパーティーだ。

タティアナ（モデル／ロメオ・ジリを着用）「全部変えなきゃ」 photo by M.L

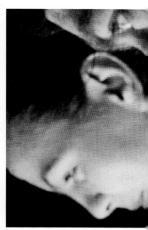

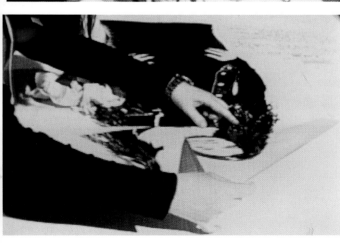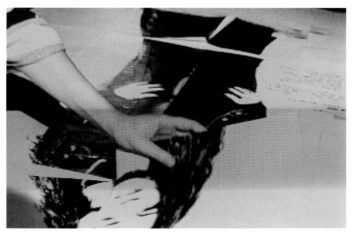

Stills from i-D Now Florence 1992 ph. Marc Lebon and Takashi Homma

BRUNO - BARBANI -
MACCHINISTA - TEATRALE

= La vera pace

what is most important in your life now?

what would you change for a better future? Ancora e ancora pace

FIRENZE

9 JAN 1992

photographer
Takashi Homm

No 102 MARCH 1992 £1.80

# i-D

i-D MAGAZINE
i-DEAS, FASHION, CLUBS, MUSIC, PEOPLE

## future now!

the science of fashion: 18-page photo special with
Joe Gatesly-Hartford
Duffy of St. George
Dirk Bikkembergs
Bella Freud
Jean Colonna
Romeo Gigli
Martin Margiela
Veronique Leroy
Christopher Nemeth

## Inner City
and Detroit's new techno generation

## David Cronenberg
the horror of 'Naked Lunch'

International cyberpunks/Techno art
Holographic fashion/Ragga Twins

USA $5.50

9 770262 357006    03

FRANCS 33 LIRE 6.900 DM 12.50 PESETAS 665 D KR 49

i-D Now exhibition, portrait of Italian worker in Florence ph. Takashi Homma    Cover of i-D No. 102 March 1992 ph. Takashi Homma

# Interna tional knit
## together

The best of Italian,
French and British
knitting. How it looks
great, and with what.
All this in unmistakable
fashion esperanto . . .

**super cardigan, great** polo neck,
long tweed legs . . .

Brighetti's terra cotta
lambswool/angora polo-neck,
this page, fine and loose,
under dark brown wide rib
lambswool/angora cardigan;
£34.95, £102.95. Dark and
pale brown checked wool
tweed trousers, by Ara,
£42. All from The Shop
at Michaela. Charcoal/
brown/pale brown leather
satchel, £69, at Loewe.
Hair, all pages, by Patrick
at Molton Brown

cardigans, two sorts,
with frilled lawn,
classic pleats

Rodier's V-necked,
sleeveless, buttoned-
through beige lambswool
mixture cardigan, this
page, with pockets,
under round-necked, thickly
ribbed, beige softest
mohair cardigan, drop
shouldered; £25, £40.
Beige lambswool mixture skirt,
£48.40. All at Rodier,
London, Guildford,
Brighton. White Swiss
lawn shirt with embroidered
collar, £38, at Essenses.
Beige suede/leather belt,
Chris Trill, £8, from
range at Harvey Nichols.
Dark brown lacy tights,
by Martyn Fisher. Shops,
sizes, colours, see Stockists

## *Italianease:* **Missoni's plaids, colours, classics not to be missed**

*Knitted mohair plaid jacket, this
page, big, loose and tied with rust
cords, to order. Rust patterned
mohair polo-neck with double
seams, plain knit sleeves, and
rust mohair skirt with vertical
knit pleats, £175. Doubled mohair
plaid, scarf, £45, and plaid umbrella, £28. Ice-blue gloves, from
range. Plaid wool coat, opposite,
gathered from shoulders, with tie
belt, over wraparound dirndl with
patch pockets, £125 and £78.
Primrose wool crepe V-necked
shirt, £50, caramel wool chalk
cable cardigan, £75. Wool gloves,
pale green ecru tights, from range.
Checked umbrella with curved
handle, as above. Fir-tree green
leather brogues on crepe soles, by
Maud Frizon, about £60. Everything, both pages, at Browns.
Sizes, and colours, see Stockists*

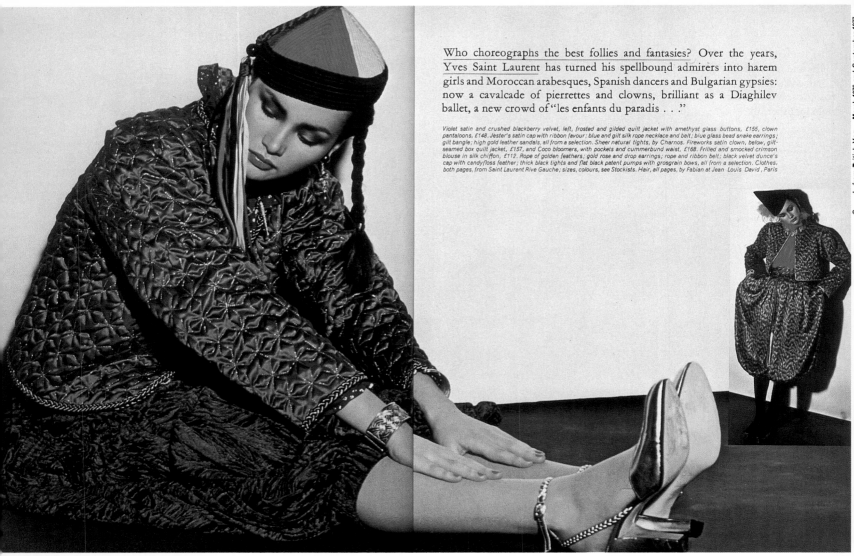

Who choreographs the best follies and fantasies? Over the years, Yves Saint Laurent has turned his spellbound admirers into harem girls and Moroccan arabesques, Spanish dancers and Bulgarian gypsies: now a cavalcade of pierrettes and clowns, brilliant as a Diaghilev ballet, a new crowd of "les enfants du paradis . . ."

*Violet satin and crushed blackberry velvet, left, frosted and gilded quilt jacket with amethyst glass buttons, £155, clown pantaloons, £148. Jester's satin cap with ribbon favour; blue and gilt silk rope necklace and belt; blue glass bead snake earrings; gilt bangle; high gold leather sandals, all from a selection. Sheer natural tights, by Charnos. Fireworks satin clown, below, gilt-seamed box quilt jacket, £157, and Coco bloomers, with pockets and cummerbund waist, £168. Frilled and smocked crimson blouse in silk chiffon, £112. Rope of golden feathers; gold rose and drop earrings; rope and ribbon belt; black velvet dunce's cap with candyfloss feather; thick black tights and flat black patent pumps with grosgrain bows, all from a selection. Clothes, both pages, from Saint Laurent Rive Gauche; sizes, colours, see Stockists. Hair, all pages, by Fabian at Jean Louis David, Paris*

# MORE DASH THAN CASH

Coat-dress £15.00
and straight skirt £9.00
Both denim, button-through,
by Reldan, at Barkers;
Harrods;
Bentalls, Kingston.
Navy blue wool sweater,
at Take 6 branches £12.95
Blue/red striped white
collarless shirt,
French Connection
at Stephen Marks,
from Cane,
170 Walton St, S.W.3 £6.95
Cashmere/wool gloves,
at Lords £3.00
Tights by Charnos.
Boots by Sacha £18.99

Hair by Sally at Vidal Sassoon.
Shops, sizes, colours,
see Stockists

art-sleeved denim jacket £11.50
atching straight skirt £10.00
Marshall Lester,
Way In.
ped cotton shirt,
larless, black buttoned,
Fiorucci £12.50
e Shetland polo-neck,
ling Cooper Jasper,
onnie Stirling;
ding Post, Birmingham £5.95
er navy tights, Charnos
wboy boots, Sacha £30.00

# SHE

**In the strange lands of the South lie mysteries we do not yet know...**

Skirt by Martin Margiela from Browns, 23-27 South Molton Street, London W1 and Liberty, 214 Regent Street, London W1; T-shirt from Oxfam, branches nationwide; shoes from local market, Mexico; wings from Camden Market, London NW1.

PHOTOGRAPHY BY CARTER SMITH ASSISTED BY BETH PERKINS STYLING BY JANE HOW HAIR BY NEIL MOODY FOR AVEDA MODEL: CAROLYN MURPHY THANKS TO ALL AT KATY BARKER AND ALL AT THE OSHO SHOT ON LOCATION IN COBA AND TULUM, MEXICO

PAT MCGRATH
PHOTOGRAPHY BY
CHAYO MATA
CO-ORDINATION BY
MICAELA TOLEDO

Jo-Ann Bromfield, 18, sales assistant at PayLess

## angels of harlem

# BLACK MAGIC

Fashion's forever shade finds fresh form. Is it in shape, shadow or silhouette - who knows the secret?

Phillip Treacy from 69 Elizabeth Street, London SW1, enquiries on 0171 259 9605; textured trouser suit by Joseph from Simpsons, Piccadilly, London W1 and Cruise, 39-43 Renfield Street, Glasgow, enquiries on 0141 248 2476; gloves by John Lewis, branches nationwide.

ph. Pat McGrath

ph. Mark Mattock

ph. Henrik Halvarsson ph. Carter Smith

Clockwise from top left: Spreads from i-D No. 167 August 1997

PHOTOGRAPHY BY MARK MATTOCK STYLING BY JUDY BLAME ASSISTED BY BECI LAMB HAIR BY EUGENE SOULIEMAN AT TREVOR SORBIE MAKE-UP BY LISA BUTLER AT STREETERS SHOT AT METRO STUDIOS PRINTING BY BDI MODELS: CLARA AT MODELS 1 AND LOIS AT TAKE 2

## i-D's essential guide to *white*

PHOTOGRAPHY BY HENRIK HALVARSSON ASSISTED BY MATILLAS STYLING BY SORAYA DAYANI ASSISTED BY ZOË KNOWLES HAIR BY STEPHEN LACEY AT STREETERS MAKE-UP BY CHARLOTTE TILBURY AT CAMILLA ARTHUR MODELS: REBECCA HARRIS AT SELECT AND JEAN-BAPTISTE AT TAKE 2 SHOT AT CLICK STUDIOS PROCESSING AT METRO THANKS TO ZIGGY AT JOHN PARKINSON

Jean-Baptiste wears pants, £140, by Comme des Garçons from 59 Brook Street, London W1 and Pollyanna, 16 Market Hill, Barnsley; high-tops, £150, by Issey Miyake from 270 Brompton Road, London SW3

an-Baptiste wears shirt, 5, by 6876 from Browns, -27 South Molton Street, ndon W1 and Aspecto, Bridge Street, anchester; Levi's 501 ans, £56, from The Levi's ore, branches natio- de; customised tie, £8, m Portobello Market, ndon W11.

"I've always wanted to innovate rather than imitate. I've been an art director for twenty years but still consider each job to be a learning experience."

Personally I am computer illiterate. I like machines but I am not mechanically minded and I have never had the time to learn. More to the point I have always had someone around who can carry out the technical stuff.
When Fiorucci commissioned me to design a range of stationery and a series of 200 stickers the job justified the expense of buying an Apple Macintosh computer. The idea of making digital imagery seemed like a natural development from the typewriter. Computer technology has increased the range of visual possibilities and speeded-up image manipulation, but I prefer to under-use rather than overkill. I wanted to mix romance with technology. The machine is programmed to do the same tricks for anybody. I like to de-program and select the mistakes of chance. I used the Apple Mac's low-tech graphics programs to produce the titles for "Rock in the 80s", a three hour documentary produced by Rapido TV. I worked with an experienced Mac operator on the animation at Decode Design Studios. Based on the concept of a ten-year clock made up of graphic shapes, we produced primitive "jumping" graphics in a couple of hours, which I then took to a video editing suit, to finish the title sequence on a Harry.
Omaid Hiwaizi, ex-"i-D" art editor: "Terry is an expert in chaos theory which is a scientific term. Terry isn't, but somehow, he gets jobs out the door. He's slowly got used to using computers but makes them fit his way of designing because he's not interested in gimmicks and effects. We had interesting moments when Terry wanted us to put paper through the printer twice for ecology's sake, but because we didn't know which side it would print we never knew which was the new version, or would overprint it twice."
In 1986 Fiorucci had been asked to stage an exhibition of rising Italian stars at Seibu in Japan. I was the only non-Italian participant, but as creative director of Fiorucci I was given honorary status and learnt to say "Buona Sera". That was how I made my first instant design exhibition, by putting together an audio-visual presentation of my past work. I made instant portraits using Polaroids and video-grabs which I manipulated on a black and white photocopier because colour Canons didn't exist back then. I needed a Japanese partner who could use a computer and joined-up with Hagime Tachibana who was a musician with the popular band Melon. Each evening we staged a two hour performance making portraits of the audience who had waited hours to see their hero Hagime. He now runs one of the best known graphics studios in Tokyo.
i-D NOW is another live exhibition event, and an extension of the magazine. i-D NOW is a situation inside a space, and a collaboration between people being creative with communication technology. The result is an interaction between documentary technology, artistic wit and image-making skills. Each event is a unique happening, recorded for

television transmission and as a printed catalogue. i-D NOW extends the barriers of print because it is not restricted by pagination or page size. It's a visual display combining sound, spontaneity and surprise.

The first event was held in Florence on 9 January 1992. At the invitation of Pitti Imagine Oltre, which is the organisation which promotes menswear fashion exhibitions in Italy, the "i-D" team created an instant installation and fashion event. We invited ten of Europe's avant-garde fashion designers and their models to Florence to be photographed by "i-D" photographers, Marc Lebon and Takashi Homma, in and around the venue, the sixteenth century Palazzo Corcini. The images were enlarged to 1.70 metre, mounted onto backing sheets and suspended on wires. Guests, press, models, stylists, designers and musicians all mixed into the photo-shoot as part of the live fashion show. Words from each person, in response to the question, 'What would you do to make a better future', were added to the originals before they were carried through the crowd and hung from the wire framework. The "i-D" team worked throughout the opening evening, giving the visitors an insight into how a design studio functions, and showing that today's computer technology and digital processes can produce exciting results almost instantly.

In 1988 we were invited to collaborate on a five day event, at Spiral Hall in Tokyo by Moichi Kuwahara, a club promoter in Tokyo. Graphically I was into Pop, Op and Surrealism, so that was the theme. Together with Steve Male, "i-D's" art director at the time, we created a series of winking banners and requested a giant egg as a centre-piece onto which we could project images from the magazine. We also asked for a fish tank, oil and water projections, fifty goldfish bowls, and a pile of novelty smiles, chattering teeth and plastic eyeballs. The event was a blast, with DJs Bomb the Base and Sarah Stockbridge doing an electric striptease, while singing with Vivienne Westwood's band Choice.

Caryn Franklin, ex-fashion editor of "i-D", presenter of BBC TV's Clothes Show: "Terry Jones is a master manipulator of image, ink and flesh. I still can't believe he mobilised a slack crew of clubbers, posers, die-hard shoppers and pretentious art students into action with such effortless ease. We would slavishly do Terry's bidding into the small hours, usually until Trish threw us out.

Terry had no room for egos and treated everyone with the same indifference. He especially didn't stand on ceremony when it came to photographers. Steve Johnston was the 'i-D' magazine straight-up king. But he was often beside himself on publication day after seeing his carefully composed imagery covered in type or colour blocks. Upon learning that one of his subjects had been accidentally (or knowingly) decapitated, and appeared headless on the page, he seized the ringing telephone and barked down the mouthpiece in angry Scottish vociferation, 'i-D hand-built by butchers'. I think Terry seriously considered that as a cover line for the next issue."

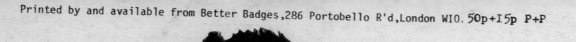

Printed by and available from Better Badges,286 Portobello R'd,London W10. 50p+I5p P+P

Is a Fashion/Style Magazine.Style isn't what but how you wear clothes. ...ion is the way you walk,talk,dance and prance.Through I.D. ideas travel ..st and free of the mainstream - so join us on the run!

WHATS IN

STRAIGHT UP:Every issue includes a report,from your open-air catwalk the street. We snap and chat to you the Model.This issue visits:The Kings R'd,Portobello M'kt. and Leicester Square.
MEANWHILE ON THE OTHER SIDE OF TOWN:Co Co the clown,the story behind the news. Theresa Thurmer,the glamorous news behind the story.
CON-FIDE:Whats going on up top,from the bottom.Steve New hides his I.D. For No I.
BACKSTABBING:What goes on behind your back.A true story featuring:Ian Melville, Domino,The Cramps and D.H.Lawrence.
DO-WHAT:Reports from the stage on which you perform-both Pubs and Clubs.In this issue:The Richmond ,Brighton.Where they make Brighton Rock.Featuring Pat or Murphy a 50's fanatic who explains why:"It's fun,sometimes agonising".
BRIGHT SPARKS:When the pressures on,sparks fly-new ideas and information.Inside: James White and the Blacks contort suits from Robot.Etc,etc,etc.
OUT OF ORDER:Off the straight and narrow:Youth walks through the supermarket doors, a short essay.

---

(i-D) PRINTED BY AND AVAILABLE FROM BETTER BADGES
286 PORTOBELLA R'D, LONDON W10. 60p+25p P+P
ALSO FROM I.D.-71 SHERRIFF R'D LONDON NW6.

Nº 2

I.D. Is a Fashion/Style Magazine.Style isn't what but how you wear clothes.Fashion is the way you walk,talk,dance and prance.Through I.D. ideas travel fast and free of the mainstream - so join us on the run.

WHATS IN

STRAIGHT UP:Every issue includes a report,from your open-air catwalk the street.We snap and chat to you the Model.This issue visits:Kensington M'kt,The Kings R'd,Blackbull R'd,Euston R'd and Camden Lock M'kt.
CON-FIDE;What happened? S.J. was sewing on buttons at the age of three. She became a Bodysnatcher-now th band has split and she admits "I'm just a hippy at heart".
MEANWHILE ON THE OTHER SIDE OF TOWN:Spandau Ballet,the facts behind the how to make it big story.The right time for Reformation.

RENT A DRESS:Girl for all reasons,lovely Jayne Cuthes explores the unknown and discovers Theatrical Costume Hire Agencies have bottomless trunks.
LONDON LOOKS:A foreign 'body'shops around for a second skin that says it all-attracting other bodies whilst fooling the antibodies.Circulate,survive.
HAT CHECK:Steve 'Mad Hatter' Jones,presents crowns he designs for the Kings and Queens of londons nightworld.Never failing to cap them all.
DO-WHAT:Reports from the stage on which you perform-where to go,what to do.In this issue:Gaz's Rockin Blues-Reggae n' Roll.A Rock n' Roll cafe "Down the Holloway R'd".Hell today gone tomorrow.An Ark Ent Event at the venue and Fr-I.D-ays thats I.D. nite when you can meet mag and pose,per- form and dance for the camera.
BRIGHT SPARKS:Ideas and information-Willy Brown a Modern Classic in profile,M's Official Secret,Acme Acting-"Doorbell rings,performance beg- ins,Karate classes-Mugger mashing exercises etc etc........
OUT OF ORDER:Wake up Albion-"Hideous visions of Eurostyle penetrate our shops"a point of view.Plus Readers Writes-A letters page......

It's deadline time, and just over a year since I wrote the
first introduction to "Catching the moment".

Acknowledgments: Big thanks to Liz Farrelly for co-
ordinating and getting this book off the ground with the
publishers, James and Edward Booth-Clibbon. Many thanks have
to go to everyone who has helped me make this book
possible, too many to name, but in the Instant Studio
alone: Kayt for her huge help with the words, Verena
Schmidmeier for organising the first plan with Kumiko
Kumigachi, Corrinna Farrow, Matthew Hawker, Kate Law, Lorna
from Latent and Inger Stanko for getting through the last
four deadlines! All the photographers and collaborators who
are included in the book and all those who I could not
include because of time and space. The writers and editors
who have made "i-D" and the other projects possible and all
the clients that have agreed to my madder ideas and become
partners in chaos. Not least, thanks to Tony Elliott who
became the saviour of "i-D" in 1984 and has been patiently
supportive throughout the years of our partnership.
Most importantly, Tricia for her passion, Kayt and Matt for
their new perspective.

Contents, to be read backwards or forwards!
Endpapers and chapter opening/closing spreads:
p.6/p.38/p.82/p.124/p.174/p.202/p.238
photographs by Terry Jones, from his personal visual diary.
Cover ph. Oliviero Toscani, Takashi Homma and Tricia Jones.

"I've been an art director now for 20 years but still consider each job to be a learning experience."

ROWNTREE'S STRONG

14/50

Terry Jones '92